JEFF FOSTER graduated in Astrophysics from Cambridge University in 2001. Several years after graduation, he became addicted to the idea of "spiritual enlightenment", and embarked on an intensive spiritual search which lasted for several years. The spiritual search came to an absolute end with the clear seeing that there is only ever Oneness. In the clarity of this seeing, life became what it always was: spontaneous, clear, joyful and fully alive. Jeff now holds meetings and retreats in the UK and Europe, clearly and directly pointing to the frustrations surrounding the spiritual search, to the nature of mind, and to the Clarity at the heart of everything.

Also by Jeff Foster:

Life Without A Centre
Beyond Awakening

THE
REVELATION
OF ONENESS

Dialogues on Nonduality
and Spiritual Awakening

JEFF FOSTER

NON-DUALITY PRESS

First published July 2008 by NON-DUALITY PRESS

Typeset in Warnock Pro 11/13.5

NON-DUALITY PRESS, Salisbury, SP2 8JP
United Kingdom

ISBN 978-0-9558290-4-8

www.non-dualitybooks.com

Out beyond ideas of wrong doing
and right doing
there is a field.

I'll meet you there.

When the soul lies down in that grass
the world is too full to talk about.

Ideas, language, even the phrase "each other"
doesn't make any sense.

Rumi

Contents

Introduction ⁊ ix

Expressing the Inexpressible ⁊ 1

DIALOGUE ONE: *The Spiritual Search*............................5

DIALOGUE TWO: *The Myth of Mind* 57

DIALOGUE THREE: *Unity in Diversity*....................... 123

DIALOGUE FOUR: *Abundance*...................................... 179

DIALOGUE FIVE: *An Ordinary Awakening* 225

One, One, One 277

Note: the transcripts in this book have been anonymised. Edits have been made to improve the clarity of the text in its translation from the original audio, and occasionally different questions and answers have been combined.

Introduction

Jesus said to them:
"When you make the two one,
And when you make the inside like the outside
And the outside like the inside,
Then will you enter the Kingdom."

Gospel of Thomas

A quiet revolution in spirituality is taking place. There is a growing sense that freedom cannot be found in philosophies, religions, ideologies; that it cannot be located in books, or reached through lifetimes of intense spiritual practice; that it cannot be passed on by enlightened or awakened spiritual masters; that it cannot be owned, cannot be taught, cannot be captured.

There is a growing sense that freedom is all there is, that it goes right to the heart of what you are, that it is constantly available and costs nothing. And that's what this message, which I call Life Without A Centre, points to – the absolute freedom right at the heart of life. It's a radical message, to be sure. And yet it's as soft and gentle as a kiss from a loved one.

This book is about the possibility that the spiritual search, and indeed all the seeking of the mind, can come to an end, once and for all. And in the absence of that search, there can be a clear seeing that all there is, is Oneness. And in the clarity of Oneness, life loses its heaviness, and *what is* is always enough. Some people have called this "spiritual awakening". But it's not something complicated. It's not reserved for the lucky few. It's an awakening as simple and obvious as the sound of the rain *splish-splashing* up on the roof. It's a bit like having a dream, and getting lost in it, and then waking up, and opening your eyes, and looking around and realising that *yes, of course, it was just a dream...*

There is no condemnation of seeking here, or of any religion or belief system. Seeking is nothing more or less than a longing for Home, a desperation to remember who you really are beyond name and form, beyond thoughts, beyond concepts, beyond all beyonds. And the search plays itself out, as it must. This is not to condemn the seeking, but to point to the possibility that it can fall away, to reveal something far more explosive than the spiritual teachings of this world ever promised.

This is not a new set of beliefs, or a fresh collection of ideas for the mind to chew on. No, this communication uses words to go beyond words, to point to something that cannot really be spoken of. It is not a teaching, not a communication from individual to individual, but a sharing from Oneness to Oneness. A sharing that ends in a revelation which completely transcends the dream of "me-and-you".

And on some level, no more words are really necessary: it is already complete. Oneness is already perfectly whole, arising presently as the chair, the floor, the table, the body, the eyes, the nose, the arms, the legs, the heart beating, the breathing. All of this is Oneness, and nothing is out of place. And yet, for the individual, perhaps this cannot yet be seen.

For the individual, there may be more reading, more effort, more going to spiritual meetings, more meditating, and more trying to understand all of this. And that's exactly as it must be. The teachings of nonduality will appear to be relevant as long as there is an individual there trying to grasp them. That is the only purpose of these words: to be there, in friendship and love, for that individual. To meet them exactly where they are.

But when that individual dissolves into clarity, when the search unravels, these pointers to the ineffable will fall away too, and there will only be the immediacy of what is, with nobody there to know it. There will be a robin singing in the tree, a car whooshing past on the road, a cup of tea in your hand, and it will all be the divine Mystery; you will never look for anything else ever again, and there will be a complete release from the burden of individuality. A perfectly ordinary life will be lived, but nobody will be living it. And, in joy and clarity, it will be seen that there has only ever been this freedom, and that all the seeking and suffering of a lifetime played out in absolute innocence.

It may help to speak briefly about my past – bearing in mind, of course, that what we call "the past" is just a memory, just a thought arising presently, and that my past is really no more special than your past, or anyone else's for that matter..

In my mid-twenties, after a lifetime of shyness, anxiety and an intense dislike of the entity I called "myself", I entered a period of deep depression and illness. Fuelled by the desire to escape the suffering of a lifetime, I then embarked on an intense spiritual search which lasted for several years, taking me on a journey through all the world's religions and spiritual traditions. For all of my life I had been a committed atheist, but the suffering had finally become so intense that an escape into spirituality seemed to be the only option.

I became addicted to the idea of "spiritual awakening", and shut myself off from the outside world, meditating and self-enquiring and constantly changing and questioning my belief systems, reading literally hundreds of spiritual books and sitting for hours at a time in my garden trying to be "present", waiting for the moment when the separate self would disappear and suffering would be no more.

However, I never found what I was looking for, and my despair and frustration reached a critical point. And then, in the midst of that despair, something opened up. The mind, exhausted from a lifetime of trying to reach unreach-able goals, collapsed, and a deep relaxation took place. And the secret was revealed right in the midst of what I'd taken to be "my life". The spiritual search ended with the reali-sation that there was only Oneness, and life was already complete, and wasn't separate from what I took myself to be. In that clear seeing, all seeking fell away, leaving only the clarity and simplicity of what is. It was a shocking to realise that the secret of spiritual awakening had been with me right from the beginning, but I just hadn't been able to see it, because I'd been too busy looking for it, and in that, separating myself from it. But the separation had been an illusion, and in the falling away of that illusion the truth was revealed, as clearly as a punch to the stomach. And the truth was revealed in a chair, a flower, a tree, my hands, my feet, everything. The revelation of Oneness had been happening all around me, in each and every moment, but in my search for an identity I'd missed it completely.

But in hindsight, how perfectly it had all unfolded. A lifetime of seeking and suffering had been necessary in order to wake me up from the dream of seeking and suffering! And in fact, the seeking and suffering had always been pointing to another possibility: they had always been pointing back Home.

At first, I just met with people in pubs and on park benches and chatted about my experiences. Then a website appeared, and books got written, and meetings started to happen, first in London, and then in other parts of the UK and abroad. I never expected any of it. The whole thing seems to have a life of its own now, and who knows how it will evolve?

It's clear that Oneness delights in expressing this message. And what a gift it is to be able to meet so many people from all over the world, and yet to see that there are no "separate people" at all, and that it's all One. Really, I'm only ever meeting myself and every question that I'm asked is the same question: it's the mind longing to come Home. What a perfect play it all is.

Well, now it's time to come Home. Read the dialogues with an open mind, and an open heart, and it may dawn on you: it was never about the words. Beyond the words, something else is happening, and it's too extraordinary to talk about.

These meetings aren't really meetings at all. They are bon-fires, in which all the questions of the mind unravel and burn up, leaving only the wonder of what is. Really, nothing can be said about this burning, because even the attempt to talk about the burning burns up in this. And yet, words continue to come, and life continues to unfold, and it's quite clear that we are not in control of this astonishing dream world, and that we are constantly being embraced by Oneness, in each and every moment, from cradle to grave, and beyond.

In these pages, may you meet your own absence, and explode into wonder.

Jeff Foster
June 2008
Brighton, UK

Expressing the Inexpressible

The Tao that can be told is not the eternal Tao.
The name that can be named is not the eternal Name.

Lao-Tzu, Tao Te Ching

Already, there is only Oneness.

Just life, but nobody living it.

Just *this*, playing itself out spontaneously, of its own accord, in its own time.

And there is no "you" separate from "this". That's the illusion. That's the dream. That's the suffering.

Only nothing – no-thing – arising as everything. Only the absolute paradox of it all. And yet, in Life Without a Centre, there are still faces, places, feelings, ups and downs. Although now the ups are *equal* to the downs, pain is *equal* to pleasure, the most excruciating suffering is *equal* to the greatest joy. Because with the collapse of the individual self comes the ending of all opposites, all opposition, all duality, which is to say that everything now exists in perfect balance, as it always *has* done.

And yet, there is nobody there to know that balance, nobody who could name it, nobody who could speak of it, even if they wanted to.

This is *grace*, and it will never be captured in words.

And yet the words come…

The mind asks:

How to use dualistic concepts to describe that which is beyond duality? And anyway, isn't "beyond duality" just another concept, perhaps the biggest concept of them all?

The mind will struggle with these dream questions. But it has missed the point entirely. The mind is so lost in the dream of time and space that it could never hope to see this.

You see, what is being said here has nothing to do with words.

Once we get tangled up in words and concepts and meanings we're so totally, completely, utterly *lost*. Because this message is about what is *presently* happening: present sights, sounds and smells. It's about the utterly obvious *present appearance* of life, an appearance which appears to nobody, an appearance which dances and swirls and pretends to be solid but actually has no solidity at all, an appearance which cannot be grasped in any way, by anyone at any time.

It's an appearance which cannot be escaped, cannot be denied, cannot be transcended, because the person who would *try* to do any of these things does not even exist.

That person is an apparition, a ghost, a mirage, a thought. And what power does thought have?

And so this is the end of choice, the end of control, and a plunge into something far more explosive.

This is the absolute freedom which cannot be reached through any sort of effort or non-effort.

This is the end of duality because it is the wide open space, the vastness in which duality appears to arise in the first place.

This is totally extraordinary, and yet it is nothing special.

This is the miracle of all miracles, and yet it is as simple as breathing.

This is death, and yet it is also the source of all life.

This is not a concept to be understood, not a new belief to be believed.

This is breathing, this is the heart beating, this is an entire world arising out of nothing and falling back into nothing, ceaselessly, playfully, like waves in the ocean, like icy breath on a winter's day, like the memory of a loved one long since departed.

This is not a state to be reached.

It is not something that some people have and others don't.

This is just a description of the utterly obvious.

And it's so simple a newborn baby could see it:

Life has no centre.

And never did.

DIALOGUE ONE

The Spiritual Search

*From wherever and whenever this insight is
communicated, it has no connection with
end-gaining, belief, path or process.*

*It cannot be taught but is continuously shared.
It needs not to be argued, proven or embellished,
for it stands alone simply as it is.*

Tony Parsons

Part One

Jeff: On some level we all have a sense of something *beyond*. Something beyond the coming and going of things, beyond who we think we are, beyond the endless cycle of birth and death, beyond our achievements, beyond our names. Beyond all beyonds, there is a sense of unity, a sense of Oneness, of wholeness.

And as very young children, as babies, we are not yet *separate* from Life, and with that there is an innocence, a very alive and very palpable sense of wonder at the world. Somehow, as adults, we lose that sense of wonder, that sense of being absolutely present, totally at one with whatever is happening. We become very solid, very heavy, full of knowledge, full of regret, full of anxiety about the future. We feel *separate* from life. We fall into duality. We talk about "me and my life", "me and my past", "me and my goals", as if we were somehow separate from these things. Unlike newborn babies, we have a very fixed idea of who we are. We cease to be amazed at life as it is. We stop *playing*. We become very complex creatures.

Now, what we are talking about today is not a new message. You find it everywhere really. All religions and spiritual traditions, in the end point to this Oneness, this Unity. And they call it God, or they call it Spirit, or they call it Energy, or they refuse to even talk or think about it.

And if you have come this far, you have a sense of what these words are pointing to. But *of course* you do, because it's not separate from what you are!

But we get very lost, don't we, in our search. In our spiritual search, as well as our material search. The mind's never ending search for *something more*. We never seem to be satisfied with *what is*, with what's happening. It never seems to be enough, and in a million different ways we try to recapture this sense of Oneness, having felt that we lost it somewhere along the way.

We were all newborn babies once; we've all tasted that simplicity, that freedom. And so to try and recapture it (although of course we don't realise that's what we're doing) we meditate, we plunge ourselves into our careers, we drink or take drugs to lose ourselves, we read spiritual books and self-help guides, we fall in and out of love, we spend our money on things we don't really need.

We spend our lives trying to come home. That's what we all want, really: *to come home, just to come home*.

What we are talking about today is the possibility that you never left home in the first place. The possibility that the sense of being a separate person is just an illusion, and that the illusion can fall away. And in that falling away, what's left is seen – in absolute clarity – to be Oneness. Yes, *everything* is seen to be that. There is nothing that Oneness is not... otherwise it wouldn't be Oneness!

And it can be seen in clarity that this whole search of ours is just a game that Oneness is playing with itself. Trying to find itself. The wave trying to become the ocean. Just a harmless game, the cosmic entertainment. And there can be so much laughter when this is seen. And in the seeing of it, it is released.

No wonder our desperate search for Oneness can only ever lead to frustration and disappointment, to a sense of *not quite being there yet*, of not quite being home, not quite being whole. Because in the attempt to *find* that, we are *fuelling* the sense of separation, the sense that we are not there already, and it's a vicious circle.

So we aren't going to be learning any new practices today. This is just a description of what there already is, of what's happening now. But the poor little mind can't see it! We can't see it! Well of course *you* can't see it! Because *you* – the individual who thinks he is separate from the Whole – don't exist! *You* are just a thought, arising now, arising *in* this!

What we're talking about today isn't about the words, and we can get so lost in words and concepts. But it's not about the concepts and it never was. But the words and concepts are fine, they are part of the play of Oneness as well. We don't need to reject the words or concepts, or reject our spiritual practices. Just to point to the possibility that perhaps *already* there is Oneness, right at the heart of things, right here. Where else would it be? And perhaps in the seeing of that, the practising and the striving and the longing will fall away, to reveal a clarity that's absolutely beyond mind.

And this isn't something complicated. It's not an *intellectual* understanding. We don't need any more concepts, any more knowledge. The amount of knowledge we have already is enough! So this isn't really about the words, or the understanding of those words, it's really about the – *and the moment you say it you've turned it into something* – call it an energy, call it a resonance, it's undeniably there when the seeking subsides. On the surface what is happening here is that a bunch of people have gathered in a room to listen to someone else talk about nonduality and spiritual awakening. But what's *really* happening here is quite astonishing: Oneness is meeting itself. And that's what it's always doing. We're just pointing back to it here. That there is no solid "you" at the heart of your life. That's the mirage, that's the illusion, that's the heaviness. There's just life living itself.

And to the mind this is heresy! The mind goes "of course *I'm* in control! *I'm* doing this! *I'm* responsible for everything that happens!" So this message can be quite threatening to a mind hooked on the idea of choice and control. But really this is the freedom of it: *Life lives itself.* We are not separate people in a room. There is only wholeness, and it constantly shines.

And some spiritual teachings talk about awakening, enlightenment or liberation, and they can make it sound like it's something you can get, given time. Something you can have. And the beauty of this, is that it's so open, so free that it can't be possessed, it can't be grasped, it can't be had by an individual. And that is the freedom of it. The frustration in the spiritual search is the attempt to grasp this, to grasp the ungraspable. It doesn't need to be grasped. It's already presenting itself. And yet, in this, the endless seeking of the mind is allowed to continue for as long as it needs to. Even seeking is allowed in this. Seeking is as much Oneness as anything else, and that's the ultimate secret really. We can spend our lives trying to put an end to seeking, trying to stop the mind, but the mind never needed to be stopped. That's the beauty of this, nothing needs to stop. Oneness embraces it all, allows it all to continue, until it doesn't anymore. And on some level this is already recognised. We've all been newborn babies. We're still newborn babies, really. Innocent, whole. We just got a little confused for a while.

So, it cannot be understood. And that's the freedom of it. That's the beauty of it. We'll open up now for questions, and comments, and apparent answers. But really this isn't about the questions and the answers. It's about something that's far too simple for all of that. And yet the questions and answers play themselves out, and it's so obvious that you're not doing that. If you could stop the seeking, stop the questioning, you would do it right now, you'd have done it already. The mind just plays itself out. This is life living itself. So all we can do with words is to try and point back to this as clearly as we can.

***Questioner*: Jeff, I recognise almost everyone in this room. We've all come many times to ask questions. You've sat and listened to us asking questions. What is the most common error that we make?**

Well, questioning is what the mind *does*! The mind wants to *grasp* this freedom, wants to *understand* it, wants to take it and *use* it somehow. So really, every question is the *same* question. Every question rests on the assumption that there is a separate person there, a questioner, and that there is an answer that you can get, and that once you get the answer, you know, *bang*! So really it's all the *same* question. Every question is the same question. It's a movement into a future. Into some sort of future understanding.

So there's no basic, fundamental *error*. Because to say that there is a fundamental error would be to imply that you could somehow correct the error, given time. That there is something *you* are doing wrong, something that *you* can fix, given time. No, nothing needs to be corrected. The assumption of a separate person is just an assumption. An assumption does not need to be corrected through effort. But when that assumption is seen in clarity, it no longer has any power. And this seeing is happening now, and it's always happening, although that could never be apparent to a separate individual.

Q. I think that's the part where I get confused. I don't feel that it's happening now. I hear you and other teachers saying that I am That, that I already know all of this, and yet I still blather on with these questions!

And *It* is what is doing the blathering. Right now! Oneness is right there, blathering away!

The questions just come out. They happen. If you could somehow correct this, if this was something you could do, if there was an answer, if someone could tell you how to correct this problem, there would be a *formula*, and you would just do it. That's the myth. That's the search. The search for the antidote to a non-existent problem.

So, there is the assumption that this needs to be seen by you, which implies a future. Well, I *tried* for years to see this, but I never could. It was only in the *falling away* of the seeking that it revealed itself.

And it's this. And it's here. And it's now.

Q. So what needs to fall away is the thought that this can be seen in the future?

Well, you could spend years trying to *get rid* of that thought too!

Q. Yes, it's circular.

Yes. The mind always wants to *do* something. It doesn't want to hear that nothing needs to be done. And that's *not* the same as saying "don't do anything". Things will be done. In fact, everything that needs to be done is already being done. Look, right now, thoughts are swirling around. *Are you doing that?* If you were doing that, you would be able to stop those thoughts right now!

You see, everything just *happens*, and this is the last thing that the mind wants to hear! It's all spontaneous, the whole thing. And you can't *reach* spontaneity. You can't reach the effortless using effort.

Q. Actually I felt that spontaneity coming here today. I didn't really want to come here, but it happened.

Yes, everything just happens. But the mind doesn't want to hear that. It wants to be in control, or at least to think that it's in control. And there can be a sense of fear beneath that. The mind fears losing its illusory control! And actually the fear is groundless. The fear is the separate person trying to cling onto control. The mind reacts against the existence of the separate person being seen through.

The good news is that there is nothing to fear. There is *just* the fear. Just presently arising fear. And the fear is just energy, aliveness, it's not really "fear" at all. It's not solid. It's a play of energy happening. And we *call* it fear. "It's my fear, I've got to *do* something with the fear." That's the illusion.

Q. And it's really only a thought?

Yes. You see, really these are not *your* questions, this is not *your* fear. This is not *your* mind. It's not *my* mind or *his* mind or *her* mind. It's all the *same* mind. It's all the same question. It's the Universe questioning itself. Any question that you could ask here, it's been asked before. You are not alone.

Every single question that arises at these meetings, I've already asked them. For years and years, I asked every single question known to man. And I never found a single answer, not one that satisfied anyway. Not one that ultimately satisfied. Answers satisfy for a while, and then the next question comes up!

Q. It all feels very unsatisfactory!

Yes, of course, because every question assumes an answer. An answer *out there*, that I can get. And that's the basic dissatisfaction. But what if *this* is the answer? *What if this - the present moment, what's happening right now, whatever you want to call it - is the answer? The answer of all answers?* That burns up all questions, and with it, all dissatisfaction at your lack of answers!

Everything that is arising is appropriate, it has to be.

Because you're not doing it. This is way too simple. To the mind, it seems almost naïve. But how can you deny *what is*? What is arising presently *has* to be arising. It must.

The mind cannot go there. But it's where you always are. It's home.

(Long silence)

To the mind this is almost madness. That everything is okay. That what arises is as it should be, because it couldn't be any other way. To the mind it sounds almost crazy. Either that, or the mind isn't interested!

To the mind, what we are talking about has no value. The mind cannot do anything with this. There is no food here for a hungry ego. This cannot be used, and that's the freedom of it.

Q. And yet the mind wants this, doesn't it? It searches. It desires. The mind has a funny relationship with this.

The mind lives in a world of things. Of duality. Of boundaries and limits. Of this and that. Of up and down, left and right, good and evil, ignorance and understanding. It tries to use the world of duality to understand that which is beyond duality. The mind thinks it can *know* this. It tries to use limitation to go beyond limitation, and fails miserably.

But the beauty of this, is that it cannot be captured in any idea, by any system of thought. It cannot be put into a box and sold. It if could, it wouldn't be freedom. If it could be captured, it wouldn't be what it is. Aliveness cannot be captured, it's too alive! And aliveness will destroy any attempts to capture it. And yet it *allows* the seeking too.

The mind will only see paradox here.

Q. The mind thinks that it knows this, doesn't it? It's very tricky. There can be impersonations of this. It can try to convince itself that it's experiencing this, when it's not.

Yes. The mind has a sense of this, but it can't do anything with it. It tries to grasp this. And it will claim all sorts of experiences. But what we are talking about is not an experience. Experiences come and go in this.

Q. So this is beyond all experience? Which is why it cannot be described, and you can only point to it?

Yes, and that's why there are no prescriptions. Nobody can tell you what to do to get Oneness, although many people will try! The moment someone gives you something to do, they are feeding the mind. That's what a hungry mind wants: something to do. Some path, some process, some more food. "Give me something to do" is the mind's mantra. And yet, having said that, there is nothing wrong with this effort. That's the mind's job and it does it perfectly. Everything performs its function perfectly. There is no blame here.

But really, all that effort can become so exhausting. Trying to grasp, trying to know, trying to achieve, trying to be free. Trying to become what you are. Trying to see what this is. And it's bound to end in frustration. Because this is presenting itself all the time, it's constantly revealing itself, and that takes no effort on your part whatsoever. And yet the efforting plays itself out, as it must.

And it's always new, always changing, but the mind can only see what it knows. It sees the past. And it might even take the words being used here today, and turn this into some sort of path, some sort of process, some sort of intellectual understanding. This is what the mind does in its innocence. In its innocence, it tries to grasp this.

Q. But it can't, can it? It's like "me" trying to awaken. I can't, because it's not "me" who awakens. The awakening is *from* the dream of "me". There's a real tension there, a real struggle.

Yes, that seems to be the paradox of this. That there is just what's happening. Sights and sounds and smells and feelings and colour and textures, just what's happening. Just what is arising presently. Just this. And *yet*, in that, there appears to be this separate "me", this person, who appears to have some sort of life *outside* of this. And to the mind that is the absolute paradox of nonduality. It cannot be understood.

In actuality, there is no paradox. The mind *calls* it a paradox because it's trying to understand it. Actually there is just the divine mystery of it all, and it cannot be known. What's happening now cannot be known, cannot be grasped. The paradox of nothing as everything, the paradox of Oneness appearing as separate things. But the mind always moves away from that absolute simplicity and obviousness of what is. It moves into a future. It moves into the story of "me".

Q. Is the paradox just the mind trying to understand something that it will never understand?

Yes. But actually there is no paradox. There is just the thought "there is a paradox". So this entire world of thought that the mind has constructed, it's gone in a flash, when the thought isn't there. When the thought goes, the world goes. That's how fragile it is, that's how precious it is. And on some level we all know this, that all the concepts in the world, all the knowledge in the world, can't bring us home. Because all of it is just a thought!

Q. When you're so used to operating in the world of thought, everything seems so solid. It's like attention has to come back to thoughts, otherwise there's a solid reality around them.

And yet the beauty of thoughts, is that they just arise out of nowhere. Nobody is thinking. There are thoughts, but no thinker. *You* are not doing thinking.

Q. But something's gone wrong somewhere?

Apparently so. It's when they begin to be *my* thoughts, that's where the problems begin for the individual.

Q. It's absurd really.

Yes, in a sense it's absurd. What the mind does is absurd. But in another sense, it's absolutely appropriate. It's what it has to do to find itself. All it's trying to do is find itself. All it wants to do is to come home. And it's doing all of this absurdity in absolute innocence. It doesn't really know what it's doing! We don't really know what we are doing. If we did, we wouldn't do most of the stuff we do to ourselves!

But we turn the mind into the enemy. We are always doing something with the mind, trying to control thoughts, trying to suppress them, putting the mind on a leash. As if you were separate from it all! As if it were yours to do something about! But nothing is yours, and that's the freedom. It all just arises out of nothing, and it's spontaneous. That's the gift of what is. And the moment there is a movement to try and possess this freedom, that's the suffering.

And yet, in the so-called material world the seeking seems to work for a while. If you want something, you can go out and get it. If you want money, you can, apparently, go out and make money. This seems to work, most of the time anyway. But the mind thinks it can use that same mechanism to get this freedom. It thinks, in its innocence, that it can seek its way to freedom, that it can somehow *find* awakening. To the mind, if it can't grasp something, if it can't possess something, then it's worth nothing. But in the absence of the looking, Oneness reveals itself. And then it's like, "oh, it was this, it was here all along!"

Q. So seeing just arises when it arises?

Yes, it's too simple. We're like newborn babies.

Q. But something is going on here. Being here reminds me of some sort of spiritual path. I mean, I could be looking to you to help me get something.

Yes, in the story, it appears as though you decided to come here. That you were drawn by something, and ended up coming here. But actually this – sitting in this room, talking to each other – is all there is. It's all that's happening. And in that, the story "I came here today" arises.

But actually, what's happening is that Oneness is meeting itself. And resonating. And you are not doing this. It's only in the *story* that "you" did this, that you are somehow responsible for being here. That's a story we tell.

You know, I could tell the story that I got the train here today. And on the level of a story, it's true. But it's just a story arising now. It's just a thought. And what's far more alive is this, what's happening. And this allows those stories to arise. This isn't about denying the stories. If someone asks me my name, I'll say "Jeff". I don't have to say "there's nobody here and I'm just a story"! So the ordinariness of this is quite shocking to a mind that's been seeking the extraordinary for a lifetime. But that's the freedom of it. It was always in the very ordinary. It was in the table. It was in the chairs. It was in the floor, the ceiling, the breathing, the heart beating. The ordinary things of life. And yet we could never see it, because we were looking for something higher, something deeper, something more meaningful than what was already the case. Something more than this.

And we'd separated the ordinary from the extraordinary, the lower from the higher. That's what the mind does, it *separates*. In its innocence, it's all it can do. So really this is Oneness meeting itself, as it's always doing. Not just at this meeting, but everywhere.

~

Q. So does meditation, or self-enquiry (asking the question "who am I?") feed the mind as well?

Well, you could ask "who am I?" until you are blue in the face. But who is asking? You see, you will never find an answer to that question. You will only ever find the asking. Just the question "who am I?" floating in nothingness. But in that sense it serves a purpose. To lead to a point of absolute frustration, showing you that the question "who am I?" is based on a faulty assumption – that there is a separate, solid "I" that can be found through effort. But there is nothing wrong with self-enquiry. If it happens, it's absolutely appropriate.

Ultimately however, no practice, spiritual or otherwise, can satisfy, because as long as there is practising, there is a *separate person* doing the practice, a *separate person* doing the meditation, a *separate person* doing the self-enquiry. So perhaps that is the point of meditation, self-enquiry, and so on: to open up the possibility of realising that there is nobody there who does any of these things in the first place.

And that is the absolute freedom that isn't a result of anything. Freedom cannot be reached through effort. But I'm *not* saying don't go off and self-enquire. You have no choice! If you find yourself self-enquiring, then that's what's happening, and that's already Oneness. It's Oneness doing the self-enquiry! That's the grand cosmic joke: it's all already Oneness. Spiritual practices are divine, as they are. There is no condemnation here, although that's how it might be heard.

~

Q. So there are no special conditions for seeing to arise? It will arise when it does?

There's only ever seeing. The miracle is all that's ever seen. This doesn't involve a future.

Q. So seeing isn't something that's going to come in the future?

It's already happening. It's all that's happening.

Q. But the seeing sometimes appears to be obscured.

There can be *waiting* for seeing. And it's just an idea.

Q. So is that idea getting in the way of seeing?

Apparently so. But actually, nothing could ever get in the way of seeing. It's just an *idea* that something can get in the way of seeing! That idea simply arises *in* the seeing, the seeing that you aren't doing. The seeing that is. What can get in the way of this? This is constantly revealing itself.

There's the idea that you aren't seeing it yet. The idea of a separate person who could see this. The idea of a person who is separate from this, who one day will see it. And the whole spiritual search begins there. That's the root of it all. Really, Oneness is all that's ever seen. All that's ever smelled. All that's ever heard. All that's ever thought.

Q. We make a big deal out of this don't we? I mean, with all our spiritual teachings.

Yes we do.

~

Q. What is the purpose of ideas getting in the way of seeing? Is it part of the play?

It's Oneness playing the game of being separate. And there is no point to a game. It's just a game, just a joyous play of light and sound and apparent thoughts getting in the way. And when the idea of being a separate person falls away, it's *all* seen to be a game. And in the game, everything is equal, everything is allowed, everything can be itself fully, but the heaviness goes out of it, the suffering goes out of it. It's a divine play, and there's nothing serious about it.

To a separate person, this existence can seem very heavy. It's a big world out there, and you need to protect yourself, defend yourself, you need to know who you are. That's the root of the whole thing, the root of all suffering.

Q. But that's part of the same game?

Yes, it's Oneness playing the game of being a separate person so it can finally come to know itself.

Q. But there is so much suffering, and it doesn't make any sense to the mind.

It doesn't make sense because the mind is trying to understand it. The mind is trying to understand a game, a dance. It's a dance! A dance cannot be understood, and does not need to be. Its purpose is not to be understood. The purpose of the dance *is* the dance. It *is* its own purpose. In itself, it is already complete. To the mind that's incomprehensible. The mind moves away from the sense of Oneness, and begins to ask "why?". When the separation falls away, that question doesn't even arise anymore.

And yet there appears to be this play of separation, and apparent people going on a spiritual search, and the falling away of separation, but it's not as a result of anything. It's uncaused. There's nothing you can do to see all of this, because you *are* all of this.

So, *why* separation? *Why* suffering? Well, the answer is always staring you in the face. The answer is this. This puts an end to all questions. The fact that this is happening *is* the answer. To the mind that's too simple. But this simplicity is very powerful. It burns everything up, and leaves only presence.

Q. Does the mind fear that?

Yes, of course. To the mind, the end of questioning, the end of me, is like death. "What will I do when I'm not there? How will things get done? If the seeking ended, wouldn't I just sit on the floor in a pool of bodily fluids and do nothing?" *(Laughter)*

These are the fears the mind uses to keep itself going, to try and cling on. And all the while, life just lives itself. As it's doing now. What's happening now is Oneness doing itself.

In that there is no fear. The end of the known is the end of fear. Because it's the end of having to defend something. There is nothing to defend. There is just openness. Just love.

Part Two

Coming back to the idea of spiritual practices, the reason I say that there is nothing you can *do* to get this, and that there is no spiritual practice that can lead to this, is that *already* it's being done. "What can I *do*?" is the mantra of the mind. And really every question is just a version of that. "What can I do?" And the mind could never see that even the asking of that question is already Oneness *doing* itself. And to the mind this sounds crazy!

If you want a spiritual practice, I'll give you one. It's being here. There you go.
(Laughter)

Whatever you are doing: sitting on the toilet, walking in the park, doing your shopping, it's already there. It's *Oneness* sitting on the toilet, *Oneness* walking in the park, *Oneness* doing the shopping. Oneness does everything. And the mind comes in and goes *"I'm* doing it, *I'm* doing it, *I'm* doing it!" It's a constant monologue, a mantra. The mind wants to feel responsible, wants to be in control.

You see, the joy of being a child is that there is no control, it's just doing itself. And there's an innocence to that. A natural innocence that we lose, because we want to play God. We want to be in control of our thoughts, our feelings, other people, and so on. But another possibility always whispers gently in the background: that it's all a dream. Oneness is doing it all. We have no choice. And there's no purpose to this play, this dream. The joy of it is *in* the playing, *in* the dreaming, and it has no purpose outside of itself.

It's the Universe playing, dreaming, seeking. The Universe being fully what it is. But we separate ourselves from it, and then we wonder why we feel separate, incomplete. And then we do so many things in order to lose ourselves. We turn to drink or drugs or meditation or work, in order to lose ourselves, to feel at home. It's a kind of addiction. The mind is an addict.

~

Q. Couldn't these activities just be Being's way of giving itself a day off? A break from the illusion of being an entity?

We think that these activities are giving us an experience of Oneness. Actually what they are doing is *destroying* us as we know ourselves.

Q. Yes but it feels great.

Of course!

Q. So we all dip in and out of this all the time, whatever the method is: drink, drugs, exercise, and so on. So we all know this already. And yet we get on the bus or train and come to these meetings. What are we doing? Are we trying to get it permanently?

Yes, we always want something *permanent*. We want *permanent* Oneness, *permanent* pleasure, *permanent* happiness. And we want it all for ourselves. And we think this is an experience that we can have. Actually when this happens, you are not there! When you're in the middle of a bungee jump, all thought falls away, and you're simply not there. And the mind comes back in and says "I experienced Oneness". "It happened to me". "I'd like to get it back". That's the search. But the beauty of this, is that we don't need to jump of a cliff with a piece of elastic tied to our waists to see it. It's in the very ordinary things too. In the smallest things.

Q. Yes, that's right, because I was thinking about an aspect of my last job. When it worked, I was in the zone, and I didn't have to try. It felt great, and I didn't have to try at all.

Yes, it's a release from the heavy burden of "me", from having to do or be anything. And in the absence of "me", things get done, effortlessly.

Q. Yes, and it's an example of where you're not jumping off a cliff, but things still get done.

This is revealed all the time. But to the mind it has no value.

Q. It does to me. I just know when I'm in that thing. I feel a quickening.

Yes but that's not the mind. It's something far beyond...

Q. What about if you're doing a really boring job? It's difficult then to make this seeing happen.

Yes, you can understand all of this intellectually, and really that intellectual understanding means *nothing* when you're sat there in your boring job!

Q. Yes that's the problem. I can know it, but not see it.

Yes, you can sit there in your boring job, and tell yourself "there's nobody here, it's all Oneness", and the job is as boring as ever!
(Laughter)

Perhaps you could tell your *boss* that there's nobody there and it's all Oneness! He might fire you, and that would solve everything!
(Laughter)

Q. Or he might not pay me, because there's nobody there to pay!
(Laughter)

Q. I was walking down the street the other day, looking around and thinking about this, and I felt really great. Then a guy walked past me and said "what are you leering at?"
(Laughter)

Q. He was very aggressive, he was drunk or something. I came back straight away to this unpleasant feeling of fear.

Yes, the mind comes back in.

Q. And I guess I could say, "well, Jeff says even *that* is it", but you know, I wanted to get away from that feeling straight away. So even the wanting to get away from it, is it?

Yes, but you can *tell* yourself that and it means nothing! This is not an intellectual understanding. All the intellectual understanding in the world means nothing, when you're faced with pain, it just means nothing. It all falls away in the face of that.

Q. So when things are unpleasant, it's alright to know *that's it*, but it's also alright to still apply some sort of technique to get you through it?

Oh, absolutely, yes! But this feeling of unpleasantness, it's just a feeling. It's energy. And the separate person says "right, this is unpleasant, I want something else, I want something pleasant." So it's the search for the pleasant, the search for something more, the search for a better situation, that's the duality. *What is* versus *what could be*. That's the suffering. To a separate person *this* will never be enough.

So, for example, you're in this boring job. When it's seen that nobody is doing the job, there's no way of knowing what will happen. It doesn't necessarily mean that you'll leave the job. You might stay. But there is no way of knowing in advance. You might find yourself walking away, that day. You might find yourself staying for the rest of your life. But the point is you won't know. Life lives itself out of that *not knowing*. It's like, "I know I dislike this job, I know I'm going to have to stay here, I know that things won't change for me." Knowledge becomes so heavy. *That's* the unpleasantness. It's the *knowing*. "I *know* this job."

Q. But when you're there with it, it's often so overwhelming, what's going on, that you forget all this. In the moment you're so overwhelmed.

And again that's part of the play. The apparent coming and going of this. The seeing and the losing of it. That's how it appears to unfold. But you are not *doing* that coming in and going out. If you were doing it, you'd stop doing it, right now!

Q. But sometimes there can be a very thin knowing, very minute, and sometimes it's very strong.

It can appear that way. And it plays itself out. The knowing of it and the losing of it. And at some point the whole thing falls away. The very idea that you can come in and go out falls away. That there's a separate *you* who can experience that. That idea falls away. And it's seen: Oneness is everything. It's even the "boring" job.

Q. So, you are patient with the job, you endure it, and that's a part of it as well? You wait to see if the unpleasantness passes? But it's like, I sit here and listen to this stuff, and then go out into the world, and then all the unpleasantness comes back.

The mind thinks this is something it can *use* to change a situation in your life. That *you* can do that. Actually when this is seen, when this message resonates, it begins to do itself. Life situations change *by themselves*. And, as

I said, there is no way of knowing that you'll be in that job next week. There's no way of knowing at all, actually. This is a plunge into the unknown, the unmanifest, the undiscovered. That sense of being a separate person who goes to work ("I am me, I go to work, I do a boring job, I go home") is the dream. And the mind thinks "I could be doing something else". That's the suffering, isn't it, that you have a *choice*. So the choice is the suffering. That you could be doing something else. Right now, you have no way of knowing that you'll ever go back to work. You could *tell* yourself that you will, but actually you don't know, you cannot know.

When you're at work, there is still just this. The same thing, what's happening in this meeting, it's the same at work, or anywhere. There's just what's happening, there's just Oneness doing itself. And that can include a feeling of boredom, a feeling of frustration. It's not *your* boredom. It's not *your* frustration. And then there's the idea that you need to get a better job. Like you have choice in the matter! And that doesn't mean that you *won't* get a better job! That's how it might be heard. Without the story of choice, it just does itself. And you might find yourself, when it's ready, when life is ready, doing something else. But you want to decide what's right for life *now*! That's the suffering. That's the duality. Life will present it when it's ready. It will give you what's needed.

So right now, you need to be in that job. In Oneness there are no mistakes, not even the possibility of mistakes. And intellectually that means nothing. You can be in your job, as bored as hell, repeating "there's no mistakes", and you're still as bored as hell! So it's not about the understanding of that. The mind just cannot see that when you're sitting at your desk, that's exactly what has to be happening, right then. That's not to say it will ever happen again, it's not to say that you won't leave the job in the next moment. But in *that* moment, that's exactly what has to be arising, because you are not doing it. You are not in control of it.

So in Oneness there are no mistakes, there are no problems. To the individual, there are! The individual could never see the perfection behind this show. Because the individual thinks he's separate from Oneness. That he has a choice in the matter. That he can play God. And the only suffering now is the idea that you have choice in this, that you can do something about this. That something *needs* to be done about this.

So consider the possibility that you're not doing this. This guy who goes to work, where is he *now*? Where is work, *now*? Where is boredom, *now*? Where is unpleasantness, *now*? This is all part of the dream.

(Pause)

Q. I can't wait until Monday morning!
(Laughter)

Q. What's the difference between an intellectual understanding and that which is not?

That which isn't an intellectual understanding cannot be spoken of. All I'm doing with these words is trying to describe as best I can what this is, what's seen over here. This isn't an intellectual understanding that I have. I tried for years to grasp this intellectually, but it only ever left me feeling frustrated and disappointed. It's only when that desperation to understand fell away that the clarity revealed itself. And it was seen that there wasn't anything to see! There was just what was happening. There is only ever what's happening. And that burns up any questions. And the aliveness of what's happening, it burns up all seeking. And it just leaves this. It leaves whatever is arising in the moment. And that's not an understanding that I have, although if you are listening to these words, it might appear as though there's a separate person here who understands all of this and can articulate it.

Q. So if there's no cause and effect, I can't see how listening to these gross approximations of what appears to happen could have any effect on dismantling the apparent stories!

If you are listening to these words with the *aim* of dismantling your story, there will only be frustration.

Q. Words uttered there are endeavouring to approximate an understanding in which stories are unravelled.

Look, the words that come out *here* are a response to *those* questions. They just come out in response to that. Actually what we are talking about is too ordinary to talk about! It may appear as though I'm trying to make you understand, to help you to get this. *But I don't see a separate person there.* Which is to say that I see that the idea of a separate person over there is just a thought. There's no need to

reject that thought. So there's no attempt here to make an illusory person over there understand this. Because I never understood this! So I can't help you to understand. Because there's nothing to understand!
(Laughter)

You know, if there's any use to these words, it's this: at some point the mind just gives up! Perhaps that's the purpose of these words. If the mind were trying to make something out of these words it would get so exhausted after a while. Because there's no substance here. Just words going round in circles. No food for the ego. But that's the only way I can honestly answer your question, or any question. But when those questions fall away, so does the confusion surrounding these words. And then these words are heard in absolute clarity, and it's all over.

Q. Repeat that.
(Laughter)

Which bit?

Q. That last bit.

I've forgotten!
(Laughter)

So, the *not understanding* is it! That's the short way of saying it. It cannot be understood. All I was left with, after years of trying to understand this, was the *not understanding*, was the unknown. And the unknown cannot be known. So that's where all these words are trying to point to, really: the unknown. And yet the words aren't really *trying* to do anything. They are just sounds. These sounds are as meaningful as the sound of the train going past outside. They are just *sounds*. A dog barks, a bird tweets, and this organism makes these sounds that you're hearing now. It's a dog barking, it's a bird tweeting. It's Oneness. Oneness sharing with itself. And that's all that's happening here. Or anywhere really. It's Oneness meeting itself everywhere. Seeing through different eyes. Hearing through different ears. Delighting in its infinite expressions.

Q. And even those different eyes aren't really different?

It's all One. And with that, this whole idea of personal attainment, of getting something that others have, that whole thing falls away, because it's seen to be an illusion. If there is only Oneness meeting itself everywhere, then that doesn't leave any room for this whole "I'm enlightened, you're not" thing.

Q. Actually, that doesn't interest me anymore, the notion of personal enlightenment. What seems to interest me is not having this sense of a burden anymore, this sense of limitation.

So where is the burden now?

(Pause)

Q. I don't know.

That's because it's not there. This search is a search for the end of a burden that was never there!

Q. But what sees it as a burden? These words are so meaningless when you try and apply them to anything. What is it that is burdened by what?

The burden is the sense of being a separate self, a separate person. That is the burden. And yet on investigation, the separate person is not there.

Q. Do we choose to do that? Do we choose to be individuals?

If we knew what we were doing, we wouldn't do it. If we had the choice, we wouldn't choose to be individuals.

Q. But we couldn't *not* be individuals either, could we? You seem to imply there is something wrong with that?

No, you're implying that! There's nothing wrong with it.

Q. But you seemed to imply just then that we could have chosen differently?

When the sense of being a separate person is seen through, the idea that anything could have been different falls away as well. That it could have been otherwise. Because *this* is all there is. Undeniably. And in the obviousness and simplicity of that, it's seen that for *this* to be, that whole thing *had* to happen as well. The past, whatever happened, it couldn't have been otherwise. And that's the end of choice.

Until then, there will appear to be choice. There appears to be choice until it is seen in clarity that there is no choice... and that there never was!

Q. So was there really a past? Apart from the story?

Where is the past now?

Q. So are you saying no?

I'm saying *where is it now*? It's a thought. It's a memory arising, or not. When it's not there, there is no past.

Q. It's hard for people to remember very strong or traumatic experiences that happened in the past. But recently, what's been happening to me, is a questioning about the word "yesterday". I sometimes think, what does that even *mean*? Yesterday? Where is it? I suppose that in that moment, I'm realising that yesterday isn't a thing.

Yesterday happens now.

Q. I mean there wasn't even a yesterday. Wednesday, what does that mean? Friday, what does that mean?

Even five minutes ago.

Q. Yes.

Five seconds ago.

Q. Well, that's too recent for me!

You'll have to work your way up to five seconds!

(Laughter)

Q. It's very strange.

It's always *gone*. The worst thing that happened, it's *gone*. It's always gone. That's the freedom of it. The very worst thing that ever happened has always gone.

Q. Ah, but the worst thing to happen is yet to come! *(Laughter)*

Touché!

The suffering comes from trying to cling on, from trying to grasp the past. "This is me, this is who I am, this is what I've done". It's all *gone*. It's all just a thought, arising now. All your achievements, everything you've ever done, all the people you've ever met, it's all a thought. That's how precious it is. That's how fragile it all is. That's how evanescent it all is.

Q. Physiologically, it's interesting, these thoughts can create strange reactions in our bodies. Thoughts almost become solidified. Memories of the past aren't necessarily *just* ideas. There can be a real physical sense with strong physiological responses. Sometimes it's hard to see that it's *just* a thought.

Yes, it doesn't feel like "just a thought".

Q. Yes, thoughts have that reality.

Oh absolutely. They appear to. But ultimately, they are only thoughts. That doesn't mean that to a person they can't feel very real. Of course they can feel real. But when it's seen that it's *just* a thought, it loses all of its heaviness, all of its solidity, and all those physiological responses go too. It all starts to feel like a dream. And that's not just poetic language. That's what it actually feels like. It all feels like a dream.

Q. Yes, it's all quite dreamlike. It's really mysterious actually.

It is.

Q. And yet, it has this impact. It's like, now. Where is "now"? We talk about the power of now, and resting in the now, and becoming present. But even the present, I mean, it's very light and mysterious. And then there's this idea of a future. Where is that? Where is the future? And yet there seems to be some sort of continuity. Something is continuing and yet, when you really look, you can't find anything.

It's the absolute mystery of it. Nothing is happening, and yet in that, there is the appearance of the character, the me, who lives his life and who apparently has a past and a future. And that plays out in the mystery. It's all the mystery unfolding. From the very beginning there has only ever been this. Ungraspable. Indefinable. It's always been the case.

And yet we get so lost in our stories, in our attempts to get this, in our search for enlightenment and liberation and awakening and our spiritual practices. But it all played itself out, as it had to. And even *saying* all of this, it's all part of the dream. The person who did all of those things, the person who was born, *where* is he? *Where* is birth, *where* is death? A moment before death, *where* is death? There is no death. There is no birth. There is only aliveness. Only this – whatever this is.

∼

Q. In these appearances, something is happening. They are only actually happening here, wherever that here is. Nothing is happening anywhere else.

It's all happening here.

Q. And thinking, it's always linked with tomorrow, with what's going to happen, with who I'm going to become. There's always some problem to work out. And there seems to be a past that I can go to. I can regret something, or be nostalgic, or wish I'd done something differently. And all of that is like another sort of reality that kind of takes me away from this.

Even the idea that there is *another* reality, it's a thought arising now, arising here, arising in *this* reality. There is no other reality. There is no "this" and everything else. That's the last piece of duality to fall away.

Q. So it's just another idea.

Yes, there is only the unknowable thisness. And it's already complete.

Q. And you were saying before about unpleasant experiences. You were talking about energy. There is just this energy, but it seems that if something is unpleasant, that's an interpretation, a narrowing down of experience. But if there wasn't that interpretation, it would just be whatever it is.

Which it is. Yes, to the separate person, there can be an unpleasant experience. What it actually *is*, is the mystery unfolding, right before your eyes. It's the Universe happening. It's the Big Bang.

Because there's nothing out there, *this* is everything. So what's happening here is the Universe. This is all that's going on, it's creation and destruction, it's the Garden of Eden and the Apocalypse all rolled into one. It's astonishing what's happening here.

Q. So the labelling – pleasant or unpleasant – it's the mind trying to *know* again. It needs to know. And the needing to know means that seeing things as they are, in their freshness, in their aliveness, gets missed.

The seeing of *this* destroys the knowledge. It puts an end to all of that confusion. To the mind that is terrifying. The mind wants to control.

Seeing this is the end of control. The mind can feel very vulnerable here.

Q. So if I'm bored, that's the mind knowing something. The mind's getting to know about boredom.

Yes. The boredom *is* the knowledge. "I know". It's *boring*.

Q. Because I know what it is.

Yes. It all comes down to that. *Nothing* is boring. It's not possible. It's too alive to be boring.

Q. Knowing that you know nothing can be quite scary. Presumably knowing that you know nothing, without the mind being involved, could be totally freeing.

Well, I know nothing, and I don't know it! There's nothing to know. Although, there is lots of knowledge out there in the world. But it's just mind-stuff. Just concepts.

This is too obvious to be known. It's happening now. What's happening cannot be captured by thought. And either you know that or you don't know it, but either way it doesn't matter!

Q. I'm getting an analogy with another dimension.

Uh-oh!
(Laughter)

Q. It seems to me that the self telling its stories, is all seamlessly interwoven with *what* is. So in that way, it seems that there are other dimensions beyond the third one, which intersect with the others. I know it sounds

very science fiction, but it feels to me a bit like that, just as an analogy.

There are no dimensions. That's the mind again, separating. One dimension, two dimensions, three. No, it's all Oneness. It's wholeness. In wholeness there are no dimensions. No separation. Those are just theories.

Q. It's the mind trying to understand something with an analogy, isn't it?

Yes. You could say that to a separate person there appears to be time and space. That *is* the separate person, the idea of time and space. The idea of *things in a world.* So you could say that in *this* arises the idea of dimensions, the idea of time and space, the idea of a person. Everything is just an idea.

In this, arises the idea of the dimensions of time and space, the idea of two, three, four, five, six, seven dimensions and beyond. So you could say that *this* is the Dimension that allows all dimensions. But I won't say that!

Ultimately, there are no separate dimensions. That's the mind cutting this up, trying to understand it, trying to get somewhere. Oneness isn't another dimension. It's the *only* dimension. Without a second.

Q. What we all experience, the me-ing and the be-ing, is seemingly a dual state, where we seem to have lost ourselves naturally. The separated self, the thing that identifies with control and choice, it seems like a ghost in the machine, like another dimension that intersects

the real one, which is the Oneness.

It thinks that it's intersecting it. It's not really doing any-thing. The separate self is doing nothing.

Q. Because it's a dream.

Yes, it thinks that it's in control. But it's doing nothing. It arises as a thought. The world of thought is the world of dual-ity. Things separate from other things. Dimensions separate from other dimensions. It thinks that there is the dimen-sion of the small self, and the dimension of the Big Self. The dimension of me, and the dimension of Oneness. But thought has created that. And thought is always dualistic.

Q. And it's always trying to be the master.

Yes. There is only Oneness. Only the mystery. It cannot be known. The whole question of dimensions, it falls away when it's seen that this separate self is just a story, an illu-sion. All these theories and analogies go with it. All the theories of mankind go with it. No theory in the world can capture this. All the teachings of man cannot touch this. So if there's two or two million dimensions, it's all just mind stuff. There are no dimensions, there's just this. Just what's happening. And it cannot be known. And it's where we always are.

Q. The mind is so tricky isn't it!

Yes, it's a naughty little boy.
(Laughter)

Q. You get a glimpse of resonance, and it seamlessly takes you on a little detour, and kids you that it's about what you just experienced. It's so tricky.

Yes, it's amazing.

Q. And there's nothing we can do.

It's astonishing, how clever it is. How subtle it can get. How subtle that grasping can get. And as it gets more and more desperate, it gets more and more subtle.

Q. A mind harried by thought, it's got no alternative but to seek refuge. In a sense the seeking is inevitable.

That's the *game* the mind plays. Seeking Oneness. Seeking refuge. It plays itself out.

Q. So many teachers seem to encourage that.

But we listen to them. We *want* something from them. You see, out of our need, we create them. It's the student *here* who creates the guru over *there*. When there's no student over here, there's no gurus anymore. There's no need for them. Then, in a sense, *everything* becomes the guru. This is expressing itself *everywhere*. The chair is doing it. The floor, the ceiling, the lights. Everything is teaching. The chair is teaching. The ceiling is teaching. The heart beating is teaching.

So really, these teachers do nothing. They are innocent. They don't really encourage anything. We go to these teachers, and we are encouraged by them. When there's no need to be encouraged anymore, that whole thing falls away, never to return. And then you will never listen to a teacher ever again. You will stand alone – but never lonely - in this dream world, and life, as it is, will be enough. That is the freedom from the spiritual search.

Q. The fly in the ointment, is that those conditions can't be brought about, can they?

Not by you.

Q. And yet that's a very subtle thing.

It's very, very subtle. And very, very obvious when it's seen.

Q. And of course in the world of time and space, cause and effect, it's very difficult to let go of the seeking.

Yes, the mind is afraid of letting go. But really, you don't need to let go of anything.

Without you, it all continues to function. Functioning in the world continues. If someone asks you your name, your name is spoken. That functioning does not cease. The story of cause and effect, and time and place and name, it goes on.

Life never needed you in the first place. There is nothing to lose, so there is nothing to fear.

Q. But in a way, you don't know anything about what happened to stop *your* search?

All I know is that the search ended in disappointment and frustration. And it was in the midst of that, that it all unravelled.

Q. But in a sense, so-called awakening is the biggest disappointment of all?

To the mind that wants something from it!

Q. *(Chuckles)* Yes.

It leaves you with nothing. And in that nothing, everything is revealed. Because there is no *idea* of what it is. Everything presents itself, and it's always new, and it's never known. Nothing can be known about this. And that's the beauty of it.

This isn't a teaching. It's a sharing. A description. Not a prescription. Not telling you what to do. That gets so dull, being told what to do!

Q. Descriptions can get dull too!

Yes, yes they can!

Q. Prescriptions that worked wouldn't be dull.

If they worked, that would be great. Have you found one that's worked for you?

(Pause)

Q. I don't even know.

So this whole thing ends in that *not knowing*. Not knowing what the hell is going on. It's explosively liberating. It's like anarchy. Spiritual anarchy. No students, no teachers.

Q. So whatever happens, happens. And that which *allows* liberation, nobody seems to know anything about that. It's always *after* the fact that they start speaking about it. Eckhart Tolle and Byron Katie for example.

Yes, and it didn't happen to "them". It was the "them" that fell away! For me, to say that something happened to me, feels like a lie. It all just falls away, when it's ready, and not a moment before. And there's no *point* at which this happens, really. It's *always* falling away. Everything's always falling. Nothing to grasp onto. A freefall into unity.

Q. It's not a permanent state, is it? That's what we are looking for. The self always wants things to be permanent. It wants everything on its own terms. It wants to experience something "beyond me". The perfect conditions, the perfect happiness.

It's a big list!

Q. And thinking is getting a bit of a bad reputation isn't it? There is an element in some spiritual teachings about thinking, that it's somehow bad. To me, it's not thinking

that's the issue. It's just another happening, another aris-ing. It's the *identification* with thinking. Whatever this grasping is, that's the issue, not thoughts in themselves. Thoughts also can be seen to be very transparent and light, appearing from nowhere and going nowhere. And in that space, they don't have a strong reactive effect. It's when thought is identified with "me", that's very differ-ent from thoughts just appearing and disappearing. So it's the identification.

Yes. It's the "me". *My* thoughts.

Q. *My* feelings, *my* hearing, *my* seeing, *my* doing.

Yes. That's it. We have the idea that everything *in here* is mine, and everything *out there* is not mine. Actually *none* of it is yours. It just arises in aliveness, in freedom. And it's the grasping, it's the identity, the identification, the idea of a thinker of thoughts, that's the illusion. Nobody is doing it. You cannot even choose your next thought.

(Pause)

Q. Can you see your present thoughts?

Even the idea of a present thought is *just another thought*. Another word for Oneness is Presence. Everything arises in Presence. All thoughts arise in that.

Q. I find myself trying to catch a thought.

Good luck!
(Laughter)

Q. Well, I think that if I caught the thought I could see it properly.

You cannot catch a thought. You can't catch a cloud. You can't catch a wave.

Q. There is a Buddhist Sutra on that. It's all fleeting. There one minute and gone the next.

Yes, *everything is changing, so nothing can be yours.* Not even a thought. The most intensely personal thought is not even yours! The breathing isn't yours. The heart beating isn't yours. It's all just happening. Spontaneously. And it's already liberated. That's the relief from the burden of having to do, having to choose. It's doing itself. It's already being done. And the mind goes "If I let go of control, if I let go of choice, I'll stop breathing! Or I'll just sit and do nothing all day." In the absence of you, everything happens, everything gets done. There is natural, intelligent functioning. And it's always been that way. We've just overlaid it with the story *"I'm* doing it, *I'm* doing it, *I'm* doing it...".

And *occasionally* in our lives things happen that we think are somehow beyond us. *Occasionally* we admit that there are some things we aren't in control of. *Occasionally* we will allow that.

Q. The irony is that when we totally buy our story, we become depressed...

And do nothing!

Q. Yes. We do that anyway.

So there's nothing to be afraid of.

Q. But it's not true that we buy our story is it? I mean, that we choose to?

In the dream, I am a separate person with a story. So in the dream, yes, we buy into our stories. Or we think we do.

Q. It couldn't be otherwise. So there's no volition. Words seem to confuse this issue.

This can't be expressed. There's no pure expression of this. Every expression is inherently dualistic. You can't have a nondual expression of nonduality. There's no such thing. So we have to use the words of duality here. If you're looking for clarity in the words, you'll be disappointed. If you're looking to use duality to escape from duality, you'll be going round in circles.

It's *not* that there is *no* choice. It's *not* that there *is* choice, either. But if we use words, we're immediately into the "is there choice or not?" game. Back and forth. And we're completely missing the point. The point is not to understand this *intellectually*. The point is a clear *seeing* of this.

And the mind will always struggle with this. So let it! Let it struggle! What's wrong with a bit of struggling? We don't have to make the struggling into the enemy. We've been trying for so long to end the struggle, and in doing so, fuelling the struggle.

And in the final analysis, the struggle isn't even there. It's just a thought, arising now.

Q. What is it that does *this*?

Nothing is doing this. To the mind, *something* must be doing this. It's the only way it can think about this. The mind is lost in the world of things, in the world of intellectual understanding and confusion. Actually, *not knowing,* the last place the mind wants to go, is very alive. It's the aliveness the mind could never see. The mind thinks it can reach aliveness through getting an answer to its questions. Actually, the not knowing is incredibly alive. And it's where we always are. Right at the heart of the mystery of it all.

Aliveness cannot be known. If it could be known, it wouldn't be aliveness. It would be a dead thing. So the freedom is in the *not* understanding, the *not* knowing, and the sinking into openness. And no words can take you there, if you are looking to be taken there! Because it's all that's happening. It's sitting on the chair. It's breathing. It's the heart beating.

Enlightenment is sitting on the chair. Right now. It's breathing, right now. It's the heart beating, right now. So ordinary. It's the last thing you ever expected.

Q. It's also standing up from the chair.

Yes, but right now there's sitting. The last thing we ever expected.

Q. (Chuckles) *So ordinary.*

Yes.

Q. Extraordinary.

That too.

(Pause)

Q. I was lost in Budapest the other day. I stopped in a little hairdressers, I needed a haircut at the time you see. There was a girl in there, she was so sweet, she didn't speak any English and I didn't speak any Hungarian. She gave me this terrible haircut, but she was so sweet and was so happy with what she'd done.

(Pause)

Is that the story? We were waiting for the punch line!
(Laughter)

Has anyone else got a completely pointless story?
(Laughter)

Q. Well, the punch line was that there was a beautiful innocence to it all, and it had nothing to do with... anything.

Oh yes, that's the beauty of it. It's completely free. It's revealed in... haircuts!
(Laughter)

In Budapest!
(Laughter)

DIALOGUE TWO

The Myth of Mind

*Groping after what is empty and chasing echoes
will only fatigue the mind and spirit.*

*Beyond awakening from a dream,
and then going beyond this awakening,
what remains?*

Deshan

Part One

What we're talking about today is the possibility that the endless seeking of the mind, its incessant search for *something more*, can come to an end.

And that's not something the mind wants to hear, because the mind doesn't really want to give up its seeking. Because in seeking, the mind is keeping itself alive. And so the end of seeking is the last thing the mind really wants, because to the mind, the end of seeking is death! The end of seeking doesn't give it anything to *do*, and the mind always seems to want something to *do*.

So what we're talking about today might frustrate the mind. In these few hours we're not going to be giving the mind anything to do, although it will try, it always does! And that's fine, that's absolutely appropriate, that's what the mind is supposed to do. We've been trying to *fight* the mind for so long, and it hasn't worked.

So this whole spiritual search – and really the spiritual search is just an extension of a lifetime's search for *something more* – rests on the assumption that there is something *wrong* here, that there is something wrong with *this*, with what's happening. And the search is always directed towards a future: a *future* liberation, a *future* awakening, a *future* enlightenment, a *future* happiness. So no wonder the mind is never satisfied: *the future never arrives!* And we're always left wanting, feeling incomplete. And yet we keep searching, searching, searching... and what do we really want but an *end* to this feeling of not-quite-being-complete?

But what the mind could never see is that it's this search, this incessant seeking, that is actually *creating* the problem, *creating* the sense of separation, of incompleteness.

The search rests on the assumption that we are individuals, somehow separate from Life, somehow separate from Oneness. And what the mind could never see, is that already *this*, what's happening now, is a perfect expression of Oneness.

And the mind hears that, and goes "it can't be that easy! This thing called liberation, it must take effort, right?" The mind uses effort for everything else, and so it thinks that it can use effort to reach the effortless, that it can find the end of seeking through seeking!

So what we're talking about today is not about any sort of effort, nor about any sort of intellectual understanding. It's not about understanding these words, or any words for that matter. It's not about taking on any new concepts, or losing old concepts. Concepts are fine as they are, you have enough of them already! We've accumulated so many concepts over the years!

So it's the last thing the mind wants to hear: that there's nothing to get, that *this* is all there is, that what's happening is all that could possibly be happening, and that right *there* is the freedom that the mind could never find through seeking.

The mind thinks that it can seek its way to freedom, that it can do something to reach freedom. That it takes effort to reach freedom. That freedom can even be reached! Which implies, doesn't it, that it's not here. And the secret is that it is here, and that it always has been, and from the very beginning there has only ever been freedom. And yet this whole search has played itself out perfectly. The freedom and the clarity have always been here, staring us in the face. And as a newborn baby you saw this. As adults we just became a little confused.

And so the mind hears this and asks "if the search is the problem, what can I do to end it?" That's a common one, isn't it? "What can I do to put an end to this incessant seeking, this never-ending search for something more? What can I do to end this feeling of incompleteness, the feeling that somehow this moment isn't... perfect?"

So this message can really frustrate the mind. And don't worry, if that's happening then it's supposed to! The mind doesn't want to give up. And don't worry, it doesn't have to!

Because actually the mind doesn't even exist. There's just presently-arising thought. That's all there is. And it arises along with the sounds in this room. The heart beating. Breathing happening. And sensations. And the feeling of your bum on the seat! And the mind going "this isn't enough!" And don't worry, it's supposed to, that's the mind's job. And it does its job very well.

So already, the heart is beating, and thoughts are arising, and there's movement in the room. *And nobody is doing it.* That's the secret. There is already a perfect expression of Oneness happening now *in this very room*, and yet we seek this perfection *out there*, in the future. And yet that's all absolutely appropriate. This isn't about any sort of condemnation of seeking. But this is about the possibility that it can all come to an end. Not as a *future* possibility though.

~

Q. You said that the concepts of nonduality don't deny any other concepts. But if I truly take the concepts of nonduality on board, all my other concepts - saying that there is a God, there is an afterlife, and so on - just fall away.

You see, *this* allows all concepts to have their place. But the mind will only ever see concepts. The mind will hear these words and take them on as concepts, but what these words are actually trying to point to is *beyond* all concepts. But the mind can only hear in terms of concepts. So actually nonduality is impossible to communicate with words. That's why I always say at the beginning of meetings that it's not to do with the words or concepts. It's in the energy of it, the resonance, beyond all words and concepts.

Q. But do concepts act as some sort of "block" to this?

There are no blocks to this.

Q. But it appears as though there are, that some blocks have to be removed.

And that's just another concept! And any answer to your question would just be more of the same. More concepts.

Q. So what is making those concepts?

Concepts.
(Laughter)

Q. But concepts seem to have a certain power.

Nothing has any power over anything else. Nobody is doing anything here. This is just happening.

Q. So is a concept just an idea, or is it something more?

Just an idea. Thought, knowledge, concepts, beliefs, ideas, stories. All interchangeable. All the same. All mind-stuff.

Q. So the mind *does* exist?

It only exists *as* thought. Presently-arising thought. No need to deny thought – it happens!

Q. So the concepts are similar to thoughts?

They *are* thoughts. But this message is not *about* the concepts. It's not about Jeff sharing his concepts with everyone else, or passing on some sort of understanding. It's a communication from Oneness to Oneness. And of course, those are just more concepts! Really they are *all* concepts! And we can drive ourselves mad trying to understand, trying to reach some sort of intellectual clarity. And the mind loves that, it gives it something to do. But it can be so exhausting too.

Q. So what is there, other than mind?

That's the mind talking! It wants to know what there is beyond the mind! Anything that can be said in response to that question is just part of the story of mind. This cannot be understood. So don't even try! This is a resonance from Oneness to Oneness, beyond the story of me and you, beyond our personal identities. It's nothing to do with my understanding or your understanding, however limited, or not, that is. An understanding is just an understanding.

Q. But "resonance" is just another word, isn't it?

Oh yes. But it's trying to point to something.

Q. What's it trying to point to?
(Laughter)

It cannot be answered. Only *seen* in clarity.

Q. But there is the implication that something needs to happen.

Yes, and this is the mind trying to "get there". Trying to reach that point of understanding that doesn't exist. There is only the *not knowing.* That is what we are, the Unknown. And yes, these questions arise in that. But they are just questions. And the mind thinks that once it gets an answer, the questions will disappear. And they don't.

But this is all supposed to happen. Why? Because it *is* happening, not for any other reason. This is what the mind *does*, it seeks understanding. And it's perfect in that. And it's nothing to do with you.

Q. You say in one of your books that you stopped reading about spirituality after this was seen. For me, after I've read one book on this it's obvious there's nothing more to read. To be honest, I find this boring. I'd rather read a book or watch a TV show on reincarnation or something.

Oh yes, to the mind this is *nothing*! Absolutely!

Q. There's no fun in this. Nothing exciting.

Oh no, this is *very* exciting! It's like being a child again! Open to the world. But to the mind this has no value, you're absolutely right. It has no value whatsoever. To the mind, what we're talking about is a waste of our precious time!

Q. To get out of this loop of suffering, is the trick just to *observe* all the time?

Well, the idea of getting out of the loop of suffering, that *is* the suffering. Because we've turned it into a problem. We've made what's presently happening into a problem, and then we try to escape that problem. And it never works.

Q. Yes, but the moment I talk about suffering I've turned it into a concept anyway, right? So the only thing left is to stay here and observe whatever is happening.

Well, it's happening anyway. And you don't need to observe it. That's part of the search: "If I observe my suffering diligently enough ... if I make enough effort ... then the suffering will end." That's the idea. But that is just another process, another future goal, and it takes so much time, so much energy. And it's actually that process which is *creating* the suffering in the first place. The idea of an escape from suffering is exactly what is creating the suffering and fuelling it. It's the idea that you can *do* something with your suffering that is keeping the suffering alive. It all implies that suffering actually exists in the first place!

Even the word "suffering" kills this. You see, the mind comes in, creates "suffering", and with that you get the identity of a "sufferer", the person who suffers. That's all in the dream story. What we actually are is an Openness in which everything happens, and this Openness doesn't mind what happens. It allows everything to happen, including the suffering. The suffering is not a problem. For the mind, that's the hardest thing to hear. That the suffering isn't a problem. And it's the search for the end of this illusory suffering that has made it into a problem.

Q. The problem seems to be the identification as the "one who suffers".

Yes. Suffering *is* the sufferer. Suffering *is* the identification. So when we try to put an end to suffering, we are caught in a loop.

Right now, *where* is suffering? *Where* is it?
(Pause)

Q. No, there is no suffering, unless I think about it. When it comes, and I identify with it, then the whole thing starts.

Yes. It's just a thought. That's all it is. Harmless, really. And it comes and goes in the Space that you are, in the Openness which allows everything to be as it is. It allows the suffering, and it allows the pain, and it allows everything, and *you* don't have to do anything. *You* don't have to allow anything! Everything is *already* allowed! To the mind, this sounds too simple. But in that simplicity is the freedom.

And I always say that a newborn baby could see this. That's how simple it is. That suffering is just a thought. And it's the identity as the "me". But it's just a thought. It doesn't need to be rejected or denied. And yet if you find yourself engaged in these spiritual practices, trying to allow thought, or trying to observe the suffering, then that's fine too, that's what's happening, and it all plays itself out like a movie.

Q. But there is *nobody* there trying to stop suffering either, is there?

No.

Q. That's where I find it quite confusing. You say that it's okay if there's the attempt to avoid suffering, but also that there's nobody there who could do that. It's like you're talking on two levels.

Yes, that's how it might be heard!

Q. Well, that's what you're saying.

Well yes, it could *appear* that way. But of course there aren't "two levels."

Q. It just *appears* that way?

Yes. It's the only way the mind could hear it! You see, it's the absolute paradox of this. There's nothing. What we are is absolutely nothing. No thing. No separate thing. No thing separate from anything else. And yet there *appears* to be this individual, this person who lives his or her life, and who has a past and a future. There *appears* to be that. But it's just an appearance, a story, a dream.

So you are nothing, and you are something. There is nothing, and there is everything. The absolute and the relative. There *appear* to be two levels, but really there aren't two levels at all. They are just reflections of each other. And the moment we talk about it, we've already moved into the confusion of words.

Q. So if we could rid ourselves of the confusion, we wouldn't need to use any words at all?

Well, that could just be another tactic. "I'm not going to use any words!" But if the words don't come out of the mouth, they'd probably carry on in "in your head" as it were. "Not speaking" is not the answer. Not using words, or not thinking, is not the answer, it's just another tactic. But it's fine. God knows, I used that tactic for a while! It didn't work.

Q. Because you got so frustrated with trying to think your way out of it, so you tried not thinking?

Yes. And of course that didn't work. It was just a denial of thought.

Q. But how do you know it didn't work?
(Laughter)

Q. But seriously, how do you know it didn't work?

Because it only ever left me with a feeling of frustration, of separation, of incompleteness. Trying to deny thought was exhausting, simply exhausting. I'd torn myself in two. I was left helpless and hopeless.

And in the midst of that despair, in the absolute failure of the mind to get what it wanted, something else opened up.

Q. Are you implying that something *did* work?

No. Nothing worked! And to the mind that can sound very depressing.

Q. Oh, I find it quite liberating!
(Laughter)

Q. You say suffering is just a thought. But what about deep emotional pain that *feels* physical? How does that relate to thought?

Well, it *is* thought. There is no separation between the mental and the physical, between the mind and the body. The mind *is* the body. So it's not that the thoughts are creating the pain. The thoughts *are* the pain. It's the same thing. Just reflections of each other. And yes, it can *feel* very real. But the root of it all is thought, and the root of all thought is the sense of being an individual, a person. So it all stems from this mistaken identity. It all stems from the "I".

∾

Q. You say the mind isn't separate from the body. But you also said the mind doesn't exist. I'm wondering about this dilemma.

There's only a dilemma if you're trying to understand it.

Q. But I can't control that, can I?

No.

(Pause)

Q. So the mind *is* the body?

Yes, they are reflections of each other.

Q. So the body is the mind too. They are equal?

Yes. So where is the body *now*?

Q. Well, I can see two arms and two legs...

So stop there. That's all there is. It's *that* simple.

∾

Q. What about physical pain? Is that just a thought too?

Well, we have to be very careful when we talk about this! Undeniably, there is physical sensation, yes. But all it really is, is energy, aliveness. And the mind comes in and calls it "pain" and makes it *solid*. And with that idea of pain, you become a "person who is experiencing pain". And then the search for the end of pain arises: "what can I do to end *my* pain?" And that's the suffering. In the pain, as it is, there is no suffering. There is pain, but no suffering.

And so, when the search for the end of pain collapses, the pain goes with it. And then you really have no words for what's happening. But it's certainly not "pain". "Pain" is a dead thing. What this is, is alive, and it's always changing, always fresh, always new. And that doesn't mean it's not "painful". But there's no suffering in it.

Q. When there's physical pain, there's reinforcement of the "I". And then it becomes very difficult, when you want to get out of it. For me, physical pain is a very difficult thing.

Yes, the pain is *enough*. It doesn't need the suffering. The pain is not the problem, the "me" is the problem, the "I" who experiences pain and who wants to be free from it, that's the problem, that's the suffering. That's the heaviness. The pain itself always arises in spaciousness. There's always a huge spaciousness around pain, all the time. The pain arises in That, and yet we condense it, we turn it into a little thing called "pain" and we want to *do* something with it. We want to manipulate pain. It doesn't ask that of you! It doesn't want anything to be done with it! It just wants to be there, and we don't allow it to be there. That's all anything ever asks of us: *just let me be here.* But we're always trying to do something with everything, always trying to grasp things and change them and make them ours, or get rid of them. Which is all fine, really. Until it's not.

~

Q. If we truly get this message today, we wouldn't need to come to the next meeting, would we? I mean, if you've done your job correctly?
(Laughter)

Well, there's no telling what will happen! If this is really *seen*, there's no telling who you'll be, where you'll go, what you'll do. You might come back to the meetings! You might become a monk, or you might become a millionaire. You might never read a spiritual book ever again.

But you know, some people come to these meetings just for the fun of it. They come here to play. To meet themselves. It's actually quite rare you know, what's happening here. This is so rare, this sort of gathering. People all over the world are telling you what to do, what to think, what to feel, how to change, who to be, who not to be. But this is a meeting in unconditional love. It's very rare, very precious.

But do come back next time!
(Laughter)

Q. Okay, but I won't use any words!
(Laughter)

Oh, I won't either, I promise.

Q. In non-conceptual terms, what is it that suffers?

In *non*-conceptual terms?
(Laughter)

Well, that's the illusion, that there is an entity that suffers. That the suffering is happening to a "me". That's the illusion, that's the dream. And a dream is just a dream. It doesn't need explaining. When you're fighting a dream, you're still dreaming! This isn't about *understanding* the dream, it's about *awakening* from the dream.

Q. Doesn't anything need to be dispelled?

That's exactly how the mind keeps itself going. It wants to keep seeking until this so-called "illusion" is dispelled. And that's the search, right there. The search for the "dispelling of the myth". And that search implies a future.

Q. But aren't you just reinforcing the myth, by implying that this can be seen?

Well, I'm not doing anything. You're hearing these words and making some meaning out of them. And that's all the mind can do, it's exactly what is supposed to be going on. These words just come out in response to your question. When the question isn't there, nothing is happening here.

Q. Are you implying that there's something *other* than mind, that can see this?

You see, I could say *anything* really, **or no**thing at all, and the mind would still say that I'm implying something by that! "What's Jeff *implying* by his silence? What's he *implying* by punching me in the face?" You see, it's the person *there* that creates the person *here*. It's the individual over there that creates the individual here. Actually, there's nobody over here. There's just a vast openness, a space in which this is apparently happening. The space in which you are apparently talking to me. That's all there is. The space in which everything happens. And that's what you are. So actually whatever you think or don't think, or understand or don't understand, is irrelevant to what we're talking about. And that's the freedom of it.

Q. But some teachers seem to promote the idea that you can get behind the story, behind yourself.

Well that's quite a comforting idea. It gives you something to do, something to aim for. It gives you a future.

Q. It's also very frustrating, because it gives you something to aim for!

Exactly. And I won't give you that, I promise.

Q. Some books talk about a moment of enlightenment. Something happens, and then there is nobody there afterwards. Was there a "Jeff Foster" before this happened?

That's the myth. That "I", an individual, am going to experience this thing called enlightenment, and then not be there anymore. That's the spiritual search. That's what I was addicted to for years. But it was a "me" looking for the end of "me", a "self" looking for the end of the "self"! Seeking the end of seeking. It's a merry-go-round.

But yes, that's the myth, and it can be a very convincing one. And you have all these so-called enlightened teachers telling you that they're enlightened. "I'm enlightened, and you're not, and here's what you can do to become like me!" So what they are doing, in their innocence and in their ignorance, is reinforcing this idea of separation, the idea that "I have something that you don't." But what we're talking about today has *nothing* to do with that at all.

Q. So there is no such moment that happens?

No. It doesn't happen in time.

Q. Because what keeps people looking for it, is the idea that there is a moment when this thing called enlightenment will happen.

Yes, and it can be fun for a while, to look for that! But really it could only ever end in absolute frustration, because it's the mind looking for something it can never have: an end to the mind. And it goes round in circles, making itself stronger and stronger and stronger, hoping that one day it will drop away!

And it might, actually. But it's nothing to do with anything that you could *do*. And it doesn't have to reach that point of absolute frustration and despair, though that could be the path for some.

Really there is no path to this at all. There's no path to where you are. And that's the liberation, that's the freedom of it.

$$\sim$$

Q. Jeff, the dream is that the "me" is permanent, when actually it's just a presently-arising thought, isn't it? The "me" that went to work yesterday doesn't really exist, it's just a memory. So really the "me" is just something that is brand new, all the time. And it's just a thought.

Yes.

Q. There isn't a permanent "me" that could do anything.

No, there's nothing solid there, nothing at all.

Q. It's just fresh every time.

Yes.

Q. And any so-called "awakening" event is really the realisation that there is no awakening, and nobody there who could awaken.

Yes, that's the paradox of the whole thing, the cosmic joke of it all. There's nobody there who could awaken.

Q. Yes, and the idea of a "me" is based on all the previous ideas of a "me".

Yes, and they all *appear* to be linked up.

Q. So "me" trying to understand, is like a thought trying to understand a previous thought! It's a loop.

Yes, and then every night in deep sleep, the "me" simply isn't there. Nothing is happening…

Q. … and then you wake up and say "I had a good sleep!" The "me" claims everything!

It claims everything for itself. And it even gets hooked on the idea of "awakening", and it thinks it can have that for *itself*. That's the cosmic joke: you cannot have it.

Q. Because there is no "me", it's just a presently-arising thought, arising with everything else. And it appears to be permanent, but that's the dream. Actually there is nothing permanent there.

Yes, we're just dream characters. And there's nothing heavy there, nothing solid. It's all so light.

Q. Would you say that if you take away the past and the future, you don't exist?

The past and future are always just thoughts. They couldn't be anything else. And yet they seem so real. But this isn't about a denial of the past and future. We don't have to get rid of our pasts and futures!

Q. So there is no past and future. But we were here two minutes before this, and if my mother phones from India

then I can pick up the phone and talk to her. So there appears to be time.

Yes, there *appears* to be time. Again, it's the absolute paradox of this. The timeless appears *as* time. Yes, there appears to be a past, and there appears to be this life story, but where is it *now*? It could only be a thought, a memory, arising in this, arising in presence. And that presence is what you are, actually. The Openness that allows everything to be, that allows this to happen now.

No effort is involved in this. Beyond effort or non-effort, what is happening presently is already offering itself to us. It's a gift. And it's always staring us in the face. And we think it takes a future to "get" this!

But if your mother calls you during the meeting, could you go outside please!
(Laughter)

Q. What about if you have some sort of scar, physical or mental, from your history? What does that mean?

It's the story of a past. And that's not a rejection of that, just to say that it's just a story. And every night when we fall asleep, we see this. When we fall asleep, what happens to the day? It just falls away. And it's *always* just falling away, really. But we cling onto it so tightly, you see. "It's *my* past, *my* future!" So there seems to be this "me" at the centre of everything. *Me, me, me, me, me! My* possessions, *my* achievements, *my* enemies. Me versus the world.

Q. But nobody is doing that.

No, this isn't about blaming anyone.

Q. So really when you talk about the "me" doing this and that, you're not speaking even an approximation of truth. I'll have to remember that.

Yes, you'll have to remember that!
(Laughter)

So this whole life of ours rests on this assumption that there is a separate "me", a separate self, separate from the Whole. Separate from Life. We talk about "me and my life, me and my past" as if we *had* a life, *had* a past. As if it was ours, as if we owned it.

Q. So the past is just a presently-arising thought? If you think about something that happened ten years ago, that's just a presently-arising thought?

Yes.

Q. And if I don't think about "ten years ago", then there is no ten years ago.

Yes, "ten years ago" only exists when you think about it. And children see this. Children know this.

Q. And whatever is happening here, this is all there is.

Yes, yes it is.

~

Q. The idea of a "me" is just a constant thought that appears here?

Yes, it appears in the space, in the openness that you are. So the story of me, "me and my life, me and my history" is just a story, a story that appears in the space that you are, in the space, the openness that is allowing all of this to happen. And actually the space is *not separate* from what happens in the space. And that is Oneness. That's what the word "nonduality" points to.

Q. And when you connect with the past and the future, that's just another thought arising here.

Yes. And they appear to be linked up. There appear to be psychological patterns and habits, trains of thought. And that's the mind searching for an identity.

Q. And that which is *aware* of this presence, is that also a thought?

Yes of course, the moment we talk about it!

Q. And even when I think about it?
(Laughter)

You can't get round it, you see.

Q. And even when I feel it, it's...

... it's nameless, wordless. The moment we talk about it we've turned it into an *it*, into a *thing*. It's not a thing, it's the space in which all things arise. And yet, even when we talk about "the space in which all things arise", we've turned it into another thing! So when we use language we can't get around turning everything into things!

Q. So the moment you think about it, the moment you sense it, it's not that.

Ah yes, it's too simple for that. It's simpler than anything you could ever imagine. It's more present than any idea of presence. It's more immediate than any idea of immediacy. It's closer to you than *any* idea. It's what you are.

Q. And any idea is just popping out of *that*?

Yes, and any idea is *it* too. And you're not doing it. It's just effortless. You can't understand what you are. And the good news is that you don't need to! I tried for years to understand what I was! All those concepts: awareness, consciousness, witnessing, presence, seeing, they just go on and on. When the confusion drops, what those words are pointing to is seen in clarity.

Q. The mind tries to get hold of "spaciousness" too, doesn't it. I mean, it hears you say things like "the space that you are" but all it sees now are objects. And so I can't *find* this spaciousness, I can't *locate* it.

Of course, because it's that which is allowing the objects

to be. And it's in the objects *too*. It's not *separate* from the objects. But the mind could only ever hear these as concepts, ideas. *Awareness, consciousness, spaciousness, presence.* The mind latches onto these concepts because it wants to understand. "Once I understand presence, once I understand consciousness... then I'll get it". And so the mind is assuming that there is something to *get* through understanding these concepts.

Q. But the assumption is very strong.

Yes it is.

Q. We seem to have learned it, picked it up from somewhere.

Yes, but as a newborn baby, *this* was still happening, *this* was still the case. Before all of that learning, all of that accumulation of knowledge, there was still only the absolute simplicity of what was happening. And *that* is the spaciousness, *that* is the openness. It doesn't need to be understood.

It includes everything. It even includes the attempt to understand. It allows that as well. It just sits there allowing everything. And of course the moment we talk about it...

Q. I can see another thought saying that I have to sink into this. That over time, I'll get it.

And that's okay too. There's nothing that isn't appropriate. This isn't a list of things that are supposed to happen, and a list of things that aren't supposed to happen.

Q. Is anything *not* appropriate?

Yes, that question!
(Laughter)

Only kidding. We are so used to receiving lists of things we should think, things we should feel. So many commandments, so many ideas of what's appropriate and what's not. So it's very rare to hear a message like this one, a message which *includes* everything.

Q. But when you say that everything is appropriate, the mind immediately comes in and says that some things simply *aren't*.

It's all appropriate because it's *happening*, and for *no other reason*. The separate person could never see this. The separate person could only ever see mistakes.

Q. Is the way we have been brought up inappropriate?

Well, your upbringing served to bring you here, now. That's what it all led up to. The result of your entire upbringing, your entire childhood is *where you are*. You are always left where you are! And the whole past is just a thought, just a memory. So in that sense, everything that happened was absolutely appropriate. *Because it happened*, and for no other reason.

Q. I won't remember much of what you've said today.

Good.
(Laughter)

It's not about the words anyway.

Q. What I mean is, I won't remember all of this in my mind, but there are bits and pieces of what's been shared in this room that have gone here (points to heart). I feel *that* will continue in the Now, in whatever Now I'm presented with. I don't know if that makes sense?

Well, it's not supposed to "make sense"! Not on an intellectual level, anyway. Yes, this has nothing to do with understanding any of these words. It's something far greater than all of that. Energetically, there's something very powerful happening here.

Q. You've said that that this is a rare message. But in a way, we're always communicating this, even on a bus.

Oh in that sense, this is *always* happening. What we're talking about is *always* happening, yes. But in terms of spiritual teachings, a lot of the time we're given lists of things to do or not do, or think or not think, or feel or not feel, and that's all absolutely appropriate, but all I can say is that over here, all of that just left a feeling of incompleteness. Because you're never quite *there*, you're never quite *good enough*.

Q. Therefore the teachings are inappropriate? You say they are all appropriate, but they do not end the suffering, so surely they are inappropriate?

Well, they *happen*. I see what you are saying though.

Q. So should we stop those teachers?
(Laughter)

Yes, let's shoot them all!
(Laughter)

Q. But you say there is nothing to learn, so in a sense we are all teachers.

Yes, there are no teachers. I am not a teacher. Which is to say that *everything* is a teacher. And not just people, but trees and flowers and carpets and ceilings and mugs of tea. The teaching is everywhere. We think it's concentrated in certain people, certain buildings, certain books, but really it's everywhere. It's the freedom that's everywhere, always in plain view, always waiting for the incessant seeking of the mind to come to an end. It's there to be *seen*, just to be *seen*.

Q. So maybe the word "inevitable" is better than "appropriate"?

What for?

Q. Well, we've used the word "appropriate", but maybe the word "inevitable" would be a little less confusing for us.
(Laughter)

Thank you!

Q. I'm only trying to help you!
(Laughter)

Q. You say you don't want to teach. So the teachings just happen?

Yes. This delights in expressing itself. Because it's not a communication from person to person, from individual to individual, it's life itself, it's a communication from Oneness to Oneness, and I'm not doing it. *I'm not doing it.* And I'm not just saying that to be clever! That's what it actually feels like. It's just effortless.

Q. What made you write the books?

I don't know. Nothing made me do it. It *happened*. And it kind of shocked me in a way, when it happened!

Q. Is it appropriate to say that this is a gradual understanding? It seems that sometimes we can discuss it in that sense, and other times we say that there is no path, that there is nothing gradual about this, that there's no goal, that nothing's happened and nobody is doing anything. And I'm trying to work out if there's a difference between *this*, and that apparent *gradual* understanding.

Oh yes, it *appears* to be a paradox. On one hand there appears to be nothing to do, nowhere to go, nothing but this, nothing apart from what's happening. And on the other hand there appears to be this person who *changes*.

And actually there is no paradox at all. The one is the

other. They are not two. They are not separate. So although this is all there is, and although there is nothing to get, the *unfolding* of the character, the individual, goes on, and it's supposed to. It's not supposed to stop.

Undeniably, in the story of the person, there is change. Sometimes, people who come to these meetings, they tell me that the very same words that a few months ago brought confusion, anger and frustration now just bring the sense that "wow, this is it!" So *something* has changed, apparently! There has been some sort of shift. So let's not deny that.

Q. Sometimes in those shifts, there can be an awareness of complete and utter vulnerability. The not knowing can become really frightening.

Yes, to the mind this can be frightening. But that fear is really just the mind trying to cling on. There is nothing to fear. Nothing at all. That's still part of the story of the mind: *something to fear.*

Q. There is nothing to fear but at times it feels like you're jumping off the edge of a cliff. But still there is nothing to fear.

Yes.

Q. But it seems like that, it appears like that. You're going from the known into the Unknown. And we're always going into the Unknown, actually. It's very exciting. There doesn't have to be fear. It's just like... wow.

Yes, it's the last place the mind wants to go: into the Unknown. The Unknown destroys the mind. It destroys it completely.

Q. To die before you die. It's very much that.

Yes, and the mind has an *idea* of what death is, of what it looks like. But death is really the Unknown, and the moment you think about it, it's known. So really there is no death.

Q. It's the death of the little self.

And an explosion into something far more exciting. But yes, there can be fear. But it's completely groundless. There is fear, but there is nothing *to* fear, nothing to be afraid *of*. The fear has no object. That's the freedom.

Q. So in a sense, the biggest myth of them all is cause and effect. I mean the way we speak, the way we relate, his mother in India ringing me…

What's his mother doing ringing you? What's going on *there*?
(Laughter)

Q. But really it's the biggest myth of all, isn't it? Cause and effect? Time and space, and so on?

Yes, the mind is lost in a world of duality: cause and effect, left and right, up and down, good and evil.

Q. Birth and death?

Yes. Ignorance and awakening too. And there's no end to it. The moment you're caught up in it, there's no end to it. You can't escape from duality using duality.

Q. So do you have a little bottle with the antidote?
(Laughter)

There's no *antidote* because there's no *problem*. It's the search for the antidote that is causing the problem. It's just duality again: problem and antidote. This is the dream world we're talking about here. And the waking up from the dream is the *seeing* of the dream, in clarity. You don't have to *do* anything with the dream. The *seeing* of the dream *as* a dream. And it's seen now, it's already seen, it's all we're ever seeing.

Q. It seems like there's two things running together. There's the person I describe myself as, the things I do and see and so on. And then there's the *real* me, who is aliveness, this moment, the knowing. And the one mistakes itself for the other.

There is no separation between them.

Q. But somehow I'm not seeing something.

Because you're trying to.

Q. Well, most of the time I'm just drifting along. Only

occasionally do I try! But when I do, on closer examination this "little self" always disappears in a puff of smoke. But it doesn't entirely disappear.

It's not supposed to!

Q. But there seems to be a real self and a dream self.

And that's still part of the dream. That there is a bigger self.

Q. Well the bigger self is the real self, which is just the Now. And you can describe it as aliveness, or thisness, or anything. And that's for real. And when you say "I exist", that's what this is.

And in that, arises the illusion of the person. And that's it. No movement is necessary from there.

Q. But I find myself telling myself to step back from this illusory self, and I find myself doing the seeking in that way. But I can't *not* do it. I tell myself that the "me" is not real. And it's an infinite regress. The seeking is just... all the time. There is a seeing through of the story, and a seeing of what is, a kind of tasting. A kind of leaving-it-all-alone. A deep knowing that I exist. I find the seeking thing very tricky. If I don't do it, I'm stuck in an illusion.

But you're not doing any of it.

Q. No.

It's playing itself out.

Q. Yes, it's just happening.

The idea that you can do something about it, or not, is the suffering, is the questioning. The idea that you have a choice in all of this, *that's* the problem. Without that, there is no problem. It's just playing itself out.

Q. This process just does itself?

Yes, it does itself. It *has* to.

Q. But if I understand what you just said, then I tell myself that I'm just *thinking* that it's doing itself, and that's more seeking.

The thinking is okay too. There's nothing that's not okay.

Q. It's like an infinite regress, and never quite getting there.

There's nothing to get. You're there now.

Q. I know that. It's like there's two parallel things. There's the story on the surface, and a deeper knowing.

So that's the paradox of it. *Stay* with the paradox. The moment you make a movement to try and solve the paradox, you're back into the confusion. There is only the paradox. Only the not knowing. I don't know a damn thing about this!

Q. Yes. I'll just sit with it.

What we are is the paradox. There is no "solution" to what we are. The search for the solution is the spiritual search. Yes, there appear to be "two" but in fact there's only ever One. The paradox of nothing appearing as everything.

Q. Yes, one is described as all objects, and the other is the space that the objects are in, plus the objects. The whole caboodle.

So stay with the paradox of that. The one is the other. There is no separation between the space and what appears in the space.

Q. The first is just the objects that are known, not the knowing...

Oh, if we're trying to *understand* this, there will only be infinite loops of thought, infinite regresses. But it's too simple for all of that. It's the absolute simplicity of this, of what's happening. And it's the absolute paradox of it. And the mind doesn't like paradoxes! It doesn't like the idea of two things apparently being true at the same time. It likes its truth nice and pure.

We are *living* the paradox. That's all that's happening here. And I don't know a damn thing about this! But that's the freedom. Right at the heart of that paradox. The freedom isn't to be found through solving the paradox. It's right at the heart of the paradox. It's here, right now. Always. And yes, the mind will play itself out, as it must. But it's got nothing to do with you.

~

Q. So the "me" isn't a permanent thing, then? The "I" that thinks it's doing something just arises with what's being done. They arise at the same time.

They are reflections of each other.

Q. So there is no prior "me" that does something else. The "me" just arises with whatever is being done or thought. It's just another thought.

Yes, everything is creating you. Take this bird up here.

(Points to little statue of a bird)

We think "I am seeing the bird", when actually the bird is creating the "me". The seen is creating the seer. The *bird* is creating *the one who sees the bird.* They arise at the same time and dissolve at the same time. And that's all that's ever happening. It's a play of seer and seen. A harmless play of duality.

Q. And the confusion comes in when there's an idea of a permanent me, a sort of background, which doesn't really exist.

Yes, it's all just spontaneous, there's nothing permanent. It's always fresh. Always.

And now it's time for tea!

Part Two

Q. Just before the break, we finished with you saying that the seeing of the bird was what was making you appear. So what we are saying is that any contact we have with anything or anybody, is what makes the idea of *who we are* appear. And that makes duality?

Yes, "me" and "you" arise together. I create you. Self creates other. They are reflections of each other.

Q. But that which we are, is always there?

Yes, it allows for all of that to arise. It allows the play of duality. It allows duality to play itself out, as it must.

Q. So, after enlightenment…
(Laughter)

Q. Look, I can't help but use those terms!

Yes you can!
(Laughter)

Q. But concepts will still happen, won't they?

Yes, but they are still just concepts. They are seen to be just concepts, just stories. Wonderful stories! But where do those stories ever get us, really?

Q. They get us to where we are now, I suppose.

Yes, it all only served to bring us here. Right where we are. Right here. This is it. And the mind doesn't like that! "What, you mean *this* is it? *This* is too ordinary!"
(Laughter)

A mind looking for the extraordinary could only ever see *this* as ordinary. A mind wanting something more could only ever see a problem here.

What the mind could never see is that it's the search for something more that's turning this – what's happening – into a problem. It's never enough! So when that search collapses, it is seen with absolute clarity that this is *always* enough. It's *more* than enough. Whatever is happening.

And then there is always an appropriate response to what's happening. And it's effortless. Our problem is that we want to be prepared for everything, we want to be prepared for every eventuality. We want to *know*.

Q. What is this mind? You speak about mind as if it's something solid, as if it actually exists.

It's just thought. Mind, thought, knowledge, belief, it's all the same.

Q. So there are thoughts...

They just arise.

Q. They arise and they say "this is not enough"?

Yes, that's all that's happening. And then there might be the effort to do something about those thoughts, to try and *make* this enough! That could be happening too. And that's just more stories.

Q. But I don't have to fight it?

No, it's not the enemy.

Q. It's not the enemy.

That's just what it does. And when that's seen it's just allowed to do what it wants.

Q. Yes.

Thoughts are allowed to arise. Sights and sounds are allowed to arise. Everything is allowed to arise. Because nobody is doing it. And we are not separate from what's arising.

That's the problem, we think we are separate. "I am a person who thinks! I am a person who thinks thoughts!" It's just not there. That person is just not there. There is just presently arising thought, and nobody is doing it. So thought is already released from the need to be anything other than what it is. There is *already* that release. For a newborn baby this is *already* the case. It's been this way from the beginning. As adults, we just got a little lost in this seeking game!

Q. When you say "seeking", you don't just mean spiritual seeking, it can be any kind of seeking, can't it?

Yes. We think that the spiritual search is somehow higher than the search for money, or pleasure. It's the same movement of thought, really. It's the search for an identity.

∾

Q. We are brought up to search. Since we were little we've been taught to search. And so, after a while, you end up trying to un-knot all those things. The knot that you tied.

Yes, and it seems that the whole world is lost in this dream. The dream of *something more*. The search for some sort of future satisfaction. And let's not forget, the search can be wonderful as well. Whilst it's happening, it can be wonderful. Until it's not! Until it no longer satisfies. And that's when this other possibility can shine though. The possibility that there is nothing to get. That there is already this wholeness, and it's right here, and it's what we are.

Q. There can be a point where you realise that nothing will satisfy, can't there? For me, there seems to be a knowing that nothing out there will satisfy. Not wealth, or status, or relationships.

Yes, and in the story, that can be very depressing!

Q. Or pregnant with possibilities. I find it quite liberating.

Oh, absolutely!

Q. It feels like a letting go. A relief.

Yes. What you are is that space, that letting go, that not knowing. That space doesn't need to know anything, doesn't need to be anything.

Q. I wasn't clear about what you were saying about that bird.
(Laughter)

Which bird are we talking about?
(More laughter)

Q. Does the bird create us or do we create the bird?
(Even more laughter)

Q. But this is an important question to me. How creation arises, and what is seeing what. For example, I look at swans, and I love them…

So in the story, you are an individual who sees the swan. You are separate from the swan.

Q. But what actually *is*?

The moment we talk about it, we are back into the *story* of you and the swan.

So, let's take a look. Back to the bird.

(Laughter)

Is it a bird, or is "bird" just a thought? Until I just pointed it out right then, where was it for you? Where was the bird?

(Pause)

Q. It seems that this is a whole area of misperception. It would be nice to break through the misperception, to end the dream.

And it's part of the misperception that you can break through the misperception! That's part of the dream. The thought "bird" is fine as it is. It's quite a useful word. To call something a "piece of toast", that's quite useful too. But is that what is really *is*? You see, the word "bird", or "toast" or any word, it's a dead thing. What *this* is, is aliveness itself. And everything is that. Just aliveness, just life expressing itself, and we kill it with thoughts, with knowledge, because that satisfies the mind. "Oh, I know it's just a *bird*, it's just a *piece of toast*, it's just a *thing....*" But all words come from the past. So we don't actually *see* it. To really *see* that thing we call a bird would put an end to you! To really *see* puts an end to the separation between me and the thing. And babies see this! Babies are not yet separate, that's why there is so much natural joy and spontaneity. And somehow we lose that as adults, we lose that sense of wonder. Because we've separated ourselves, we've got all our knowledge, our theories, our belief systems and complex philosophies, but we've lost our innocence, we've fallen from grace. And all that knowledge is wonderful, but it can't give us what we want, which is freedom. Because freedom is what we are.

Q. But we didn't separate ourselves?

No. Do you think we'd have chosen to do it if we had the choice? This all happened in absolute innocence. There's no blame here. There's nobody who is responsible for this. It's just how it unfolds.

∾

Q. I'm not quite sure what you mean when you say we can "see" this. Do you mean we can see it as atoms moving around?

Oh, no, it's so simple. It's already seen. Everything that needs to be seen is *already* seen. Everything that needs to be heard is *already* being heard. It's happening now. To see it all as atoms would just be another conceptual overlay.

∾

Q. You mean there is no separation, but the mind comes in and labels, and says "that's a bird", and simultaneously it's created a "me" that sees the bird?

Yes, and that means we don't have to *see* it anymore. We can turn our heads away and say "I don't need to see it, I know what it is, it's a bird!" So we stop *seeing*. And life becomes very dull, because we've already seen everything, we already know everything.

Q. Yes, because the mind has separated and labelled, and said "that's a bird".

Yes. Perhaps it's more obvious with people. When you think you *know* someone, you stop *seeing* them.

Q. That's right.

We know them. Or we think we know them. And then there's a heavy burden of *past*. And we carry that around with us, and project it onto them. "I know you, I know what you said to me, what you did to me…." And it goes on and on. And the *seeing* of that is the ending of it. And the seeing is to meet someone exactly where they are. In freshness, in openness, in aliveness. And it is seen that they are not separate from you. There is no separation, and yet the story of separation continues to function. The me and the you, those stories can play themselves out. But really, it's seen that they are just stories.

And what we are is Oneness, and that's all that's happening. That's all that's ever happening, even in this room. It's just a play of Oneness. And those apparent characters, those apparent individuals, can carry on talking and sharing ideas. But what's *actually* happening is really quite extraordinary.

Q. So this is going on all the time.

Yes, not just in this room.

Q. And the "me" thought tries to claim it all. "I did that, I saw that". But actually it's just something else that's appearing presently. Actually there's just seeing. There's nobody there who sees, and there is nothing to see.

Yes, and of course then we get into the whole language thing. *Seeing* implies someone there who *does* the seeing. But let's forget that for a moment! In that clarity, in the freshness of present seeing, where there is no separation, right *there* is the freedom, and it's where everything arises.

And there is this undeniable play of apparent separation, and we can function in the world using that, and it's wonderful, but really it can't ever give us what we want. We can't find freedom through the separation. The freedom is in the seeing-through of the separation. In the falling away of the search.

Q. Yes, and the thought "I see" doesn't see. It's just another thought that comes up along with everything that's seen.

Exactly. And so, for example, the thought bubbles up: "I see the bird, I see it, I'm doing it". Me, me, me, me!

Q. Yes, but the thought isn't seeing the bird. The bird is just seen. But there's this extra bit that says "I'm seeing the bird". It's the false I, the false me, which is just a presently arising idea.

Q. I get the sense that birds are really quite *apparent* when you see them. In the sense that this bird in front of me evokes my awareness in precisely the same way as my awareness beholds the bird. And hence the bird creates me, just as I create the bird, and each of those two points of view that you choose to focus on is a matter of

attention and perspective. And if I want to give the most accurate account that I can give, it's that here and now, the bird is being seen, *and that is me.*

(Pause)

And everything arises in that intimacy. There is no "me and the chair", "me and the bird", "me and you". There is just the intimacy. Just Oneness seeing itself, everywhere.

Q. But when we say that the bird is creating me, that is not even true either.

Ultimately nothing we say is true. This is about as close as we can get using language!

Q. It's just a thought arising here.

Yes. It's really too *simple* to be communicated. It's not too *complex* to be communicated, it's too *simple* to be communicated!

Q. Jeff, you said that you know nothing about this, but you seem to know everything!
(Laughter)

I don't know *anything* about this. There's nothing to be known about this. This is the Unknown. We are just exchanging ideas and concepts here. What this *is* cannot be known. This is the *freedom* from having to know, having to do, having to be. Oneness reveals itself constantly in everything, and it's doing it now, and it's always doing it. It's the cosmic joke: freedom is always there. It just sits there, and it waits, and it allows this whole search to go on, and the incessant goal seeking of the mind, it allows it all. And it doesn't try and stop anyone from seeking!

Q. But is this something that you know?

It could appear that way, if you are listening to these words! But really I am bewildered by it. You see, it may appear as though there's a certain clarity of expression here. But it's because I've done that whole search. Any question anyone could ever ask, I've already asked it. Every single question.

Q. The Oneness, the Omnipotence, can never be explained. It's far beyond any words, any explanation.

Yes, and the beauty of it is that it embraces all words, it allows all words to be. And when that is really seen, it all ends there. Then everything is just allowed. It's just complete intimacy. Complete not knowing. And yet in that, life doesn't stop.

Q. It *is* life.

It *is* life.

Q. Is there seeking?

Where?

Q. In life?

In which life?

Q. In your life?
(Laughter)

Seeking for the next meal, probably!

Q. What about future planning?

Make plans. But you can never know.

Q. Living in the present moment, I'm wondering if I even *need* to make plans?

If you find yourself making plans, then that's what is supposed to happen! That's the idea, isn't it: if you lived fully in the present, then you wouldn't ever need to make plans. But that's just another concept, another idea of what the present moment is. What I find is that planning *happens*. And of course, I can't know what's going to happen in the next moment, or in the next week or year. And yet, in the not knowing, plans can still get made. Planning can still happen, for a future that never arrives!

Q. I've often wondered about what you just said. I mean, if you really surrender to the present moment, whether or not there is a need to plan. I think maybe you can plan, but you don't allow it to consume you in the present moment.

But it can be seen that you're not doing any of it. If planning happens, then it's just effortless. And actually there is no present moment. Because that would imply a present moment separate from a past and future moment. So already we are in the language of separation. The present is not separate from the past or the future. So the present actually embraces all of that. It allows the apparent past and future, and planning and remembering to happen. It's the space in which everything is allowed to happen, where everything is allowed to be exactly as it is. And it's always here. It's not to be found at the end of a long search.

Q. Would you be able to work for a multinational corporation?
(Laughter)

Are you offering me a job? Is this a job interview?
(Laughter)

Q. I wish I could!
(Laughter)

Q. But would you be able to work in a job that's based on the principle of being an individual, you know, needing a mobile phone, a car, a house? When an individual

becomes like you, would that all fall away?

What I find is that in this seeing a lot of that stuff just falls away. The drive to succeed, the drive to be *someone,* just falls away. It's not a rejection of that, it's a natural movement away from those needs. It all just falls away naturally. And actually, having said that, you could see this and still be a very successful businessman. But over here, it's all just fallen away. So no thank you, I won't take the job!
(Laughter)

Q. But you haven't heard the salary package yet!
(Laughter)

Q. Sometimes there is a clarity, and there couldn't be the slightest doubt. It may just be a second's experience, but there couldn't be the slightest doubt whatsoever about anything. And then the clarity disappears. And then it comes back, and then disappears, and comes back again. So there seems to be this coming and going.

Yes, there can be. That's a common story. You're right, the clarity is so *obvious.* And then the mind comes back in and calls it clarity, and says "that happened to *me.* I had it and I lost it." And that's the mind talking. It's the story of having-it-and-losing-it. The mind wants to possess this.

Actually, what "happens" in that clarity is that *you are no longer there*! And that's so obvious too. And then the mind comes back in. And what the mind is doing, is just playing itself out, as it must. But this apparent in-and-out game eventually just falls away. It exhausts itself. It's the mind dying.

There's a beautiful symmetry to this. It plays the in-and-out game for a while, and then it just gives up. And the clarity allows all of that too. It allows the in-and-out. Apparently having it and losing it. It's all happening in the clarity.

You never *had* the clarity, ever. The clarity *is*. It *is*. And it's this and it's now. You can't *have* this. I can't have this. Nobody can have this. Ever. That's why it's free. Nobody can possess clarity. Nobody can own freedom.

Q. It's such a curious thing. Right now, it's so obvious. It's absurd that there is anybody! There is no centre. And yet then the "I" comes in and tries to recreate this. "Right, there was no centre…"
(Laughter)

Q. "Well, actually, maybe there *is* a centre…"
(Laughter)

Yes, the mind can't handle the simplicity of this. The innocence of it. And yet there is a kind of beauty to it, the way the mind tries to grasp this. To grasp what it cannot have. And it all just plays itself out, in innocence. It has to.

Q. It seems there is a common path. Hearing your stories, and the stories of other nonduality teachers, all you people had glimpses of Oneness. I heard those stories, and thought, "I've never had those glimpses". But one

year ago, I went to a nonduality meeting, and walked out in a state of shock! I then began comparing myself to those teachers...

Oh, this has nothing to do with Jeff Foster or any other so-called "teacher" of "nonduality". It's not something that I have and that you don't. That's all in the story of apparent individuals.

It's the individual *here* that creates the individual *there*. It's the person *here* that creates the person over *there* who had some sort of glimpse of Oneness. When there is nobody *here* there is nobody *there* either. And those stories of enlightenment, of awakening, of glimpses of Oneness, they are all seen to be meaningless in a way. They are just stories. There is no longer the comparison between "them" and "me".

No individual can have this. I don't have this. That's the spiritual myth, that there's a higher or deeper "state" that some people have attained, and that you can work your way towards it by following a certain path. That myth always leaves you feeling *not good enough*, somehow incomplete. But that's all in the story of individuality, and what we are talking about today has nothing to do with that, although it acknowledges it and allows for it.

Really, individuality is just the story of a past. So it doesn't actually matter what story arises, because a story is just a story, a harmless presently-arising idea. What we are talking about can be seen without any experience of spirituality. I know of a guy who worked in an Irish pub, and he just saw this, without any background in spiritual teachings whatsoever. So there's no path.

Q. This is what I wanted to hear!
(Laughter)

Haven't I said that about five hundred times?
(Laughter)

Q. Yes, but I just needed to hear it once more!

Q. Actually, I knew that guy who worked in the Irish pub. He's a very ordinary guy. I got to know him quite well, and he had no history of spiritual seeking at all. But this seems to be a rare phenomenon, you know, someone who hasn't had a particularly spiritual background.

Although, that makes it seem like a very exclusive club, to say it's a rare phenomenon...

Q. It's like you said earlier, you get to a point where you see that the seeking isn't working, and you're so dissatisfied that you get to a point where you start to look for something else. So maybe none of us are special. Or perhaps we are all special, as it were. And that's what takes place, that total *fed-upness*. The mobile phones and the jobs in the multinational corporations aren't working anymore!
(Laughter)

But those *do* work!
(Laughter)

~

Q. Jeff, from reading various books, what seems to come up often is a discussion about paths. People who are searching seem, at some point, to have an experience where they think they have understood, or believe that they know what it's about, and then about a year later they realise that actually they didn't know at all, or and something new has come up, or there is a new understanding. Is that misinterpreting what I've read? From reading your book (*Beyond Awakening*) there is the famous part about the seafood salad...

Tuna!

Q. Yes, the tuna salad! But wasn't there a period before you saw this...

The moment you think you've seen this, you're still in the story. Because *you* cannot see this. *I* cannot see this. This is the seeing-through of the whole you-and-me game. "I've seen this! I've lost this!" That's the whole back-and-forth game the mind loves to play. In the story of the person, that's all that can happen. Getting and losing. Grasping.

This is beyond all of that. When it's over, it's over. And then you wouldn't ever say to anyone that you've seen this. Outside these meetings, I rarely talk about this.

Q. There's nothing to talk about.

Yes. It's a very ordinary life. And if anyone wants to talk about this, I'll talk to them. But there's no *need* anymore to talk about it. I don't go round telling people that I've seen this, that I'm somehow special. That's all ego-stuff. And so a very ordinary life is led. But in its ordinariness... it's extraordinary. Because it's all there is. And there's no possibility of anything more. That was always the suffering: the possibility of escape. But it's so clear now: in *this* there are never any problems.

Q. Still, there seems to be a tradition of associating this, what we are talking about, with great wisdom. Why does that story still linger on? Throughout time, it's been considered holy. There are people who allow themselves to be called Your Holiness, and I just wondered what sort of nonsense is going on there. Because this seeing, this freedom, from the people I've come across, has got nothing to do with wisdom at all. One or two people I know, who've seen this, are as stupid as anybody else!
(Laughter)

Q. I mean, you speak very clearly about this, but I don't see any great wisdom from you.
(Laughter)

Damn! I went through all this effort!
(Laughter)

Q. The point is, is that this has nothing to do with wisdom, in any sense of the word.

No, it's got nothing to do with *anything*! That's why it's freedom. It's unconditional.

Q. So I don't have to laugh at your humour?
(Laughter)

No, you don't have to laugh at my humour! You know, there's great wisdom in not knowing a damn thing.

Q. So that is the wisdom?

That is the wisdom.

~

Q. Jeff, I read that Ramana Maharshi had surgery without any anaesthetic. It lasted for four hours or something. Is that possible? He didn't see the suffering. There was pain but he didn't mind the pain.

I don't see the point though! If there's something available to take away the pain, then why not? There's nothing special or spiritual about experiencing pain. Ramana Maharshi wasn't special, he was just showing us what is possible. And it's possible for all of us. It's not something that he had, it wasn't a special state that he was in. And I think he went to great lengths to try and tell us that. But we couldn't hear it. We can't hear the teachers who tell us that there is nothing to get. Until we hear them!
(Laughter)

(Long silence)

Q. So strictly speaking there's no cause and effect?

No. There's the story of cause and effect of course. It's a

story we tell. But nothing is causing anything. It's a spontaneous play. A spontaneous arising.

Q. So it's kind of… good, really?

It's freedom. It's the freedom that you are. Throughout the whole seeking game, it's always been there. And it has lovingly allowed the seeking to play itself out. It never resisted anything. It allowed your whole life to unfold exactly as it did. And it's allowing it right now. It's allowing what's happening now in this room.

Q. Is that the grace?

It's the grace that you cannot have. It's the grace that's always there. It's the grace that we are. And the moment we try to grasp the grace, try to get it for ourselves, we lose it forever. Grace is always happening. It's all that's ever happening. You wake up in the morning and there's grace, you brush your teeth and there's grace. You go to the toilet and there's grace.

Q. She's a busy woman!
(Laughter)

I knew someone was going to say that!
(Laughter)

You take my punchlines!
(Laughter)

She's a lovely woman. She allows everything to happen, as it happens. Including the most intense suffering. That's the secret. The grace is right there at the heart of the most intense suffering. It's incredible. Just think of Jesus on the cross. In the midst of the most intense physical suffering known to man, there was God, right at the heart of it. God at the heart of things: we're not talking about anything else here. It's that which allows *this* to happen.

And that's what's happening today. It's not about the questions and the answers.

Q. But also, it's a pure myth isn't it, the notion of God on the cross?

In what sense?

Q. In the sense that it's a story of the past.

Yes, in *that* sense it's a myth, and everything is.

Q. Jeff, when you walk through a park, and you've got a shadow, it looks like the shadow is moving alongside you. But the shadow doesn't really move, does it? It's always a fresh shadow, and the "me" thought is like that. It seems to be a permanent thing, always moving into a future, but it isn't really, is it? It's always a freshly arising thought, every time, not linked to previous thoughts. It's like when you think the shadow is moving, and it actually isn't. The shadow itself is a fresh shadow every time.

Yes. And so when we try and control thought, it's like fighting a shadow. Thought trying to end thought is like fighting a shadow. And it can seem so convincing, that these are *my* thoughts, that I am somehow responsible for them.

Q. Yes, it's the illusion of a me, isn't it?

Yes. Thoughts have nothing to do with you. That's the freedom, right there. You don't own them. You don't own anything. Everything already arises in this clarity, the clarity that you are. And so when we try to do something with thought, we are just doubling up against ourselves.

Q. Yes, we say "my shadow" but it's really nothing to do with us at all.

Yes, it's just shadow boxing!

Q. So are you saying that which is reflecting the shadow is as meaningless as the shadow itself?

I think so.
(Laughter)

I'm a bit confused by your question, actually!
(Laughter)

Q. Would you say that what we think we are, is no more significant than a shadow?

Yes, and we try and *do* something with the shadow! It's not the case that I am a person who has thoughts. That's the illusion, that there is a thinker, a me, an entity that's doing the thinking. *Nobody* is doing the thinking.

Q. That's just one of the thoughts, isn't it?

Yes. And we get so attached to our spiritual teachings, and we believe that we have to put an end to thought, or at least observe it properly. We believe that we have to do something with it, that we have to see it in the right way or something, in order to reach peace, or presence, or whatever. So we've torn ourselves in two, fighting a shadow, something that's simply not there. Because the thinker and the thoughts are one. There isn't a separate entity doing the thinking. The thoughts *are* the thinker.

Q. So this body-mind constellation is no more significant than its shadow.

Yes. And it all arises in the space that you are, in the space that allows the shadow. And in the final analysis the space is not separate from the shadow. It is all One.

Q. But do we have more substance than the shadow?

No.

Q. What about the shadow of the bird?
(Groans and laughter)

Q. With certain practices, like mindfulness, it seems as though you get very real results. You get moments of clear seeing, and there is a great satisfaction that comes

with that. So there is still value in pursuing these things, in the sense that they give a great deal of satisfaction.

But satisfaction comes and goes. And underneath it all is the longing for closure. For the ultimate closure, which cannot be found through any practice. That's what the mind really wants: to come home.

Q. But until such a time when the mind stops seeking, what better activity could you engage in? That's all I seem to want to do.

Oh absolutely. This isn't about any sort of denial of any spiritual practice. I'm not rejecting any of it. It's all absolutely appropriate, absolutely necessary, until it's not anymore!

Q. I think you're lying when you say that spiritual practices are appropriate.

Oh, they are. In a sense, everything is appropriate. Everything rises to meet a need. As long as there is a separate individual who needs spiritual practices, the practices will be there. There is a perfect balance to this Universe. It would be ridiculous to single out spiritual practices as inappropriate. But when the individual is no longer there, the spiritual practices fall away, because they have nobody to cling to anymore.

Q. But don't they fuel the sense of being an individual who can attain awakening or enlightenment or liberation? In that sense, they can be very ineffective.

But they are absolutely *appropriate*. In other words, if you find yourself doing these things, then that's absolutely what's supposed to be happening in that moment, because ultimately nobody is doing it. It's Oneness playing, playing at being a person who practises, or not. Already, Oneness is doing all of this.

Q. I think that spiritual practice, like any other practice, is what you make of it. I am reminded of an old Taoist story: after you've managed to find a boat, and crossed the river, you don't have to keep carrying the boat on your back.

Exactly.

Q. And whoever seeks God in a special way, will gain the way and lose God, who is hidden *in* the way.

That's exactly it. So even the spiritual practice is God.

Q. Jeff, you speak a lot about thoughts. Thoughts appear to arise from "me" as opposed to "you". So there *appears* to be a pattern to it. There *appears* to be a person behind it all.

There *appears* to be continuity, yes. There *appears* to be. It *appears* to be personal.

Q. But why is it not all random? Why does there seem to

be a pattern to it all?

That's the beauty of this. The unity at the heart of it all. A unity which *appears* as diversity. Anarchy appearing as order. The One *appearing* as the Many. It's Oneness *appearing*. Playing. Appearing as apparent individuals, living their apparent lives, with apparent pasts and futures.

And the individual who is looking for Oneness could never find it, because the individual is already a perfect expression of That. Perhaps the individual cannot see that yet. But that's okay too.

Oneness is all that's happening. It's all that's ever happening. It's all that's happened here today.

DIALOGUE THREE

Unity In Diversity

*As It Is, life has no meaning beyond itself.
It is always at the point of completion and,
simultaneously, as fresh as the morning dew
at the dawn of creation.*

Leo Hartong

Part One

What we are going to talk about today is the Unity, the wholeness that binds all the things of this world. The sense that somehow it's all One, although it appears as though there's separate people and things. And this is where all religions begin and end.

There is the possibility that the sense of being a person *separate* from the whole can fall away. The sense of being a solid "me" in the world can be seen through. The idea that you are a small self in a big world, that can fall away. And then, what's left, is just Oneness. As it always *has* been. There has only ever been Oneness, that's the cosmic joke here. What is left, is what there always was. But we couldn't see it because we were looking for it. Seems so simple, doesn't it?
(Laughter)

And of course the mind can be very threatened by this message. The mind wants to be in control, wants to know. But this cannot be known, and that's the freedom of it. You cannot *have* this. You cannot *have* Oneness, because already it is all there is.

So on the surface, what's happening here is a meeting. A bunch of people in a room , listening to someone else talk. But what's really happening, of course, what's always happening, is that Oneness is meeting itself, and resonating. I always say that this cannot be understood.

To the mind, this whole thing is a paradox. Nonduality, or

whatever you want to call it, is one great big paradox. That there's nobody here, there's no separate me, and yet there *appears* to be. What you are is nothing. What you are is an absence that allows the world to be, that allows this to happen. And yet in that absence, there appears to be the presence of a me, a self. The absolute paradox of nothing appearing as something, of emptiness appearing as form, of an absence appearing as a perfect presence. That's why I always say this is not to be understood on an intellectual level, which is to say it cannot be understood at all. There is no other level!

But what can happen, is a resonance. And it's not a resonance passed from me to you, passed from separate person to separate person. It's a resonance from Oneness to Oneness. In this sharing, Oneness resonates with itself, and that's all that's happening here. It's not about the words. But the moment we talk about it, we've made it into something. But it's not a thing. But I'm guessing that if you've come here to listen to these words, you have a sense of what I'm talking about.

This is about the possibility that the seeking of the mind can come to an end. Not through any effort of yours, though. The effort to end the seeking is more of an effort than ever. Believe me, I tried! For years! Nothing needs to end. Oneness embraces everything, it doesn't require anything to stop.

And in the absence of the separate person, life doesn't stop. It goes on but it's seen in clarity that nobody is living that life. Life has no centre. To the mind that's a kind of heresy. "Of course I'm doing this! I'm in control of this! I'm a per-

son, I chose to come here today, I chose to sit on this chair and listen to these words, and later I'll choose to go home, or perhaps in five minutes time I'll run out of the room, screaming!"
(Laughter)

Please don't, by the way.
(Laughter)

You see, life is already living itself, and this is the last thing the mind wants to hear. And of course it cannot hear it.

But whether or not the mind hears this, this is all that's happening. Oneness is already arising, as the heart beating, and breathing happening, and sounds swirling around… and the mind goes "I'm breathing! I'm hearing! I'm thinking! I'm doing it!" But if you were doing the thinking, you'd be able to stop right now.

Thoughts just arise. Isn't this obvious? Sounds just arise. The heart beats by itself. Breathing happens. It's a spontaneous play. So when this feeling of being a separate person is seen through, it's all just seen to be energy. Light. The heaviness goes out of it. It can be exhausting to be a person, to feel like you have to hold up a whole world! It's a collapse into the not knowing, into the mystery of it all. This cannot be known. And yet, in this absolute not knowing, everything happens. This is happening! It's happening now!

And yes, this message can sound very frustrating for a mind looking for something to do. Looking for a practice. But this message does not condemn any practices. Practices can still go on in this. This can be seen, and all sorts of spiritual practices can continue. Meditation can go on, self-enquiry can go on. But it can be seen in clarity that nobody is doing them. Nobody sits down to meditate. Nobody asks the question "who am I?". It all happens in absolute openness, and there is nobody at the centre who is in control. Or perhaps the need and desire to do these things will fall away. Perhaps you will find yourself never asking "who am I?" ever again. Perhaps that question will become meaningless for you, and there will just be a life living itself, effortlessly. And in that, anything can happen.

So, in the absence of seeking life is seen to be a great play. It's a play. It's not a cold detachment from the world. It doesn't mean that you sit back and do nothing. That's a common misperception. No, you don't sit back and do nothing. But you are no longer separate from it. And in that, everything gets done. Everything that needs to be done, gets done. And everything that doesn't, doesn't. The simplicity of it is stunning. And it's seen that you are not doing any of it. That you have no choice in it. It's effortless. And free.

The separation is the violence, that's what falls away. And it's seen with clarity that there is no life outside of what's happening. This, here, now, is life. This is the only life. It's always unfolding all around us, but we cannot see it, because we are too busy seeking. To the mind, this is just a room full of people. We're just a bunch of people sitting in a room. The mind cannot grasp this. There's nothing here of value for the mind. No substance, no content. And paradoxically that can be the most liberating thing. The mind says "give me something to do! Give me something to do!" And eventually it exhausts itself. The seeking is undeniably exhausting. It can be fun for a while, of course. But ultimately it's exhausting.

And even if you found what you were apparently looking for, you'd still be a separate person, a separate person with the thing that he wanted! But that's the suffering, being a separate person. So even for a separate person who *has* what he or she wants, there's still that underlying sense of separation, and that's the root of all suffering. So getting what we want doesn't really do the trick. No wonder the seeking can go on for a lifetime. But this is done in complete innocence. We don't know any better. This has been the way humans have functioned for thousands of years.

Oneness just sings from every pore of the Universe. And it's happening now. It's fully here. Not just in this room, but everywhere. Anywhere. So if this message leaves confusion, then *great*. That's how it should be. It's the attempt to understand this that is causing the confusion. The attempt to understand this *is* the confusion. And the mind goes "I'm a confused person, I need to understand this, then the confusion will go away". And that's how it keeps the confusion going.

So if there is confusion happening, then that's exactly how it should be. Nobody is doing that. You are not doing that. If you were doing the confusion, you would put an end to it right now. It would be that easy. But the history of the world suggests that it's not that easy. If you were doing the seeking, you would stop right now. But you're not doing it. And that's the freedom. It's just a play of the unknown. And to the mind that's terrifying. The mind wants to know what will happen. It craves a future. This is a plunge into the unknown. The last place the mind wants to go. But it's where you always are. It's here, right here.

This is not about questions and answers. And yet the questioning and the answering plays itself out, exactly as it must. But every question implies that there is an answer. That *this* isn't the answer. That what's happening isn't enough. And yet, that's fine too. The thought "this isn't enough" is just a thought anyway. A thought arising in this. So, let's see what happens.

Q. Could you tell us how the awakening happened for you?

It's always happening.

Q. But there must have been a moment when it happened for you.

After years and years of really intense seeking, after years of meditation and self-enquiry and questioning of thoughts, all that was left, over here, was despair and frustration. I wanted the awakening and enlightenment that I'd read so much about. I wanted peace, and I never seemed to be able to reach that place. What I could never see back then though, was that there was a separate "me" looking for all these things. I wanted awakening and enlightenment, but I wanted them for "me". And it was the "me" that was the burden, it was the sense of being a separate person that went right to the heart of my frustration. I was trying to end the self using the self. Trying to end thought using thought. I was lost in these vicious circles of mind. Seeking the end of seeking was more seeking than ever.

And it exhausted itself. You cannot awaken. I cannot awaken. There is no such thing as an awakened person. You see, this is *already* fully awake. There is only awakeness. And it's the individual, the person, who thinks they are separate from that, and out of this separation, they seek awakening. All this seeking is doing is fuelling the sense of being separate.

So the individual asks "when will I awaken?", as if it's something that can happen to "me"! But you are just a thought. The individual, who could awaken or not, is just a thought arising now. Your entire life, your life story, your past and future – it's just a thought. *And a thought doesn't need to awaken.* That thought is already arising in Oneness. And in the *seeing* of that, there is a clarity that an "individual" could never attain.

You see, the question "how can I awaken?" can never be answered. *The spiritual search is the search for the answer.* When it's seen that the individual who asks that question is just a thought, that and all questions fall away. It's a plunge into not knowing.

Actually awakeness is that which asks the question. Oneness is asking that question. You are not doing it. The question "when will I reach Oneness?" is being asked, already, by Oneness. Oneness disguised as "you", pretending to want answers to your dream questions!

131

Q. But when the identity drops away, it drops in a moment, doesn't it?

That's what drives the search, the idea of a moment of awakening. And then there's a *search* for that moment. "When will that moment come?", we ask.

Q. But did the clear seeing, when it happened, happen in a moment? That's the way I've heard it described.

It's beyond time. You know, that's what I was looking for, that moment of falling away. But as long as I was looking for it, there was a separate "me" looking for it. And as long as there was a separate "me" looking for it, there was frustration. I was locked in a world of time and space. It was in the midst of that frustration that it all opened up.

Q. So you were in the *midst* of frustration, and then there was clear seeing?

Yes, but it was seen that there was only *ever* clear seeing! Clear seeing is all that's happening. This, right now, is arising in clear seeing. But it can be obscured, apparently, by the seeking game. When the seeking game falls away, the clear seeing, which is ever-present, is revealed. It's the cosmic joke really. Oneness is fully present, right now, but we cannot see it as long as we're looking for it. But the seeking game plays itself out, until it doesn't anymore. And the idea of choice is the only suffering in this.

Q. I experience my life, especially when listening to you

and listening to this message, as a here-ness, and that here-ness is awakeness and awareness. And each person who asks a question has this sense of hereness. And the experience of being a separate person is built onto that, and believed. And although one speaks about the absence of a separate self, that can sometimes be confusing to me, because the overriding experience is one of realness. Although there isn't a separate person, there is something undeniably real about the experience of being here, of reality. Or is that just another conceptual overlay?

Well of course the moment we *talk* about it, we are using concepts. We can call it Oneness, hereness, nowness, whatever. And of course it's not about the words. So call it whatever you want, *it's all there is.*

Q. Yes, awakeness is all there is.

Yes, we can call it awakeness. So the individual looking for awakeness will never find it, because they never lost it. It's been there right from the beginning.

Q. They were only ever that.

Yes. Right from the start.

Q. I've got a funny image of the seeker, going round and seeking like mad, and suddenly stumbling across his own absence.
(Laughter)

Yes, it's the cosmic joke. And yet it plays itself out perfectly. Oneness pretending to be two, pretending to be separate, in order to find itself. It's a game. And to the individual, it can all seem very heavy. The seeking can get very heavy. There can be a real desperation to it. "I've only got a limited amount of time on this earth, and I need to awaken before I die!" That can get very serious. But the cosmic joke of all of this, is that the individual already arises in the most perfect awakeness, the most perfect presence. It's all there is. That's why some teachers call awakening the booby prize! You gain nothing, and lose everything, but in that loss is a clarity and an effortlessness that could never be reached by a person seeking it.

Q. Why is it that some apparent individuals aren't interested in reality?

Because this isn't something that they can have. The mind is only interested in something it can have.

Q. But everyone you see, they all have that reality. Some apparent people simply aren't interested. People we encountered coming here on the train, for example.

On the train?

Q. Yes, on the train.

Oh you'll find a lot of people on the train who aren't interested in this!
(Laughter)

Q. It's just that I am puzzled as to why individuals aren't interested in their own reality.

(Pause)

Q. Maybe they don't need to be.

That's it. They don't need to be. There's nothing out of place. If they're not interested, they shouldn't be.

Q. You mean it's appropriate?

Absolutely. Otherwise this becomes a religion you see.

Q. Right, right. And then this wouldn't be freedom, because they wouldn't be free to be what they are.

Exactly. This freedom allows that. It allows everything. It allows ...

Q. ... disinterest?

Yes.

Q. Because otherwise it becomes a religion and it's no longer free?

Yes.

Q. But religions are okay as well. And presumably lack of freedom is okay.

Of course.

~

Q. Jeff, we've already said a bit about spiritual practice. A lot of nonduality writers and teachers these days...

Are you calling me a nonduality teacher?
(Laughter)

Q. They say that spiritual practices don't serve any purpose because there's nobody there to do the practice. Would you say that when the seeing through occurs, it's a matter of grace?

The moment we talk about "it" happening, the mind latches onto that and wonders when this grace will happen. It's grace in the sense that it's free. It can't be had. It can't be possessed. It's already screaming from the walls, from the ceiling, from the chair, and the moment you want it you can't have it.

And in terms of spiritual practices, this is *not* about giving them up. They fall away of their own accord. Or this could be seen, and spiritual practices could continue. But the *seriousness* goes out of them. They regain their joyfulness. Everything does. Because everything is allowed to be itself, fully. So spiritual practices are allowed to be spiritual practices, but there's nobody there anymore trying to *get* something from them.

Q. Which presumably is why you find some people who are self-realised continuing their spiritual practices, and others who don't?

Yes, but there's no way of knowing what will happen. It just unfolds of its own accord, in its own time.

That's how this message could be heard though: that there's nothing to get, so you should give up. But that would be to miss the point *entirely*.

∾

Q. Yes, this has gone through my mind. If there's nothing to get, what should I do? What is there to do? It seems like a paradox.

Yes. Some people refer to this as the "Traditional Advaita" versus "Neo-Advaita" debate. To practise or not to practise? To follow the traditions or to leave them behind? If everything is perfect, what is there to do, right? If this is all there is, what use are spiritual practices? But you see, those questions arise from a complete misunderstanding of what the word "Advaita" points to.

It's *not* that there is nothing that you can do. And it's *not* that you should give up what you are doing, because that's also how this may be heard. The point is, there is no "you" who can choose either way.

In other words, *it's doing itself.* Already. So the reason I don't give out any spiritual practices is because *I don't know.* I don't know what is best for you. And anyway, you already have the practice you need.

Q. It's this.

It's this. Oneness cannot be practised. And when that is seen in clarity, the whole thing falls away. And you could call that "awakening" if you wanted to.

So that's why I don't give out particular practices, and not for any other reason. And that's also why I would never tell anyone to stop practising, as if they had a choice. What happened over here is that the practices fell away when it was seen that there was nobody there practising. I would sit for hours and meditate, and there would be a constant question: "who the hell is doing this?" And during the self-enquiry, the question was always "who the hell is doing this?". I never found anyone there doing any of those things. Perhaps that is where all these practices lead to in the end.

And so the practices just fall away of their own accord. Or not, actually. There's no prescription here. There's no way of *knowing* what will happen when this is seen. And really, *this* is always the practice. Whatever you find yourself doing, is always the practice that you need in that moment.

You see, it's always already doing itself. It's already practising through you. The miracle is already happening. And the clear seeing of that destroys the whole Traditional Advaita versus Neo-Advaita debate, which is just another intellectual game the mind plays to keep itself alive. How the mind loves its intellectual games. How the mind loves to be right. How the mind, in its innocence, loves to cling to its traditions, its religions, its beliefs, and criticise those who don't do the same.

You see, it's already complete. And it's nothing like you ever thought it would be. Who would have thought awakening would be *this*? Who would have ever thought?

Q. Every time I hear that, the question is: what's the *difference* then, I mean, if there's nothing between you and I? Teachers often say "I'm the same as you". So what's the *difference* then?

That question has fallen away.
(Laughter)

I never got an answer to that! There is no answer.
(Laughter)

This is absolute equality you see. There's just Oneness. And in that, different stories arise. The Jeff story, the John story, the Mary story. It's Oneness playing. Playing the role of different characters. We are *being played*. We are *Being* playing.

Q. There's this one thing, about the "I" thought being a mistake. But it's not a mistake, is it? It's consciousness seeing itself. Playing. But there's something, isn't there, about not being good enough, in human beings?

The separate person will never be good enough. There's no hope!
(Laughter)

Q. Or too good.

Yes, that's the same movement really. The same thing. I

mean, the ultimate version of not being good enough, is not being awake yet. Not being enlightened. Not being present enough.

(Long silence)

～

Q. Can I ask a question? You talk about the "I" thought. Something I heard which resonated was "look for where the I thought originates". But I'm not sure if that can be answered.

Yes, you are only ever left with the *looking*. That's the illusion, that it originates from somewhere, from a point. That there's an entity there. That there's *something* there. And the *real* point of self-enquiry is that it will eventually end in frustration, because that point cannot be found. And even if you think you've found it, that's just a thought: "I've found it". You've found it, so what? That isn't the origin. There is no origin.

The illusion is that the "I" originates from somewhere. It comes out of *nothing*, and that nothing can never be found. It's not part of the world of time and space. So seeking the source of the "I" could only ever end in despair, but perhaps in the midst of that despair something else can open up. The space that opens up there is very powerful, and very alive.

The "I" comes out of nowhere, of nothing. It comes out and dances. And it's not the enemy. For years I tried to get rid of it. And what I couldn't see was that in trying to end it, I

was strengthening it. It was an I – a very strong I – trying to get rid of an I!
(Laughter)

"I'm going to end the I! I'm going to do it!" I mean it's funny now, but at the time it was deadly serious!

～

Q. I find that when difficult thoughts come up, I often believe them.

Yes, and the suffering is seeing them as *your* thoughts. That *you* are doing it. Thoughts are not personal, and that's the hardest thing to hear. The mind doesn't like spontaneity!

Thoughts just come out of nowhere, and dissolve back into nothing. Like clouds passing through the sky.

Q. But they feel very real.

Yes, they can do. But you are not doing it. If you were doing it, you would stop those thoughts. You wouldn't think them.

Q. I wouldn't want the pain.

Yes, you wouldn't want the pain. Which shows that you are not doing it. Thoughts just arise, and the mind goes "these are my thoughts, they are about me, I need to do something with them". And that's the resistance to what is. That's the suffering.

Actually, the thoughts don't need that. They don't ask that of you. They don't ask to be manipulated, to be condemned, to be controlled. Nothing asks that of you. Things just want to arise and dissolve of their own accord. They just want to live, and be left alone. But the mind can't keep its grubby hands off anything.

Thoughts just come and go. They arise out of nothing, stay for a bit, and dissolve. The mind latches onto them. That's the heaviness. That's the depression. "I need to do something with these thoughts!" It's always grasping. It doesn't want to leave anything alone. It wants to dominate, to control everything.

Q. When you say that, it sounds like the mind is influencing things, that the mind is doing something, that makes me feel responsible, and that's where I get a bit confused. I've heard it said many times that everything just arises, but on another level I don't believe that.

Oh, you can't *believe* it.

Q. Yes, and that's where I get stuck.

It's an incredibly convincing illusion. For example, are you choosing to move your hands, the way you just did?

Q. I wasn't aware of it. But it seems that at other times I do choose.

Yes, it's a very convincing illusion! The illusion of choice. It's amazing. Amazing. And you can't understand it. Nobody can understand it. It cannot be understood. To the mind, a full understanding of this would be like death. And that's the last thing it wants. So you don't want to understand this, really! Nobody wants to.

To the mind this is death. Death of control. Death of choice.

Q. It's terrifying.

Yes. To the mind, death is the end of "me". The end of my control over the world. The end of choice. That's why we fear death and illness. Because they show us that we don't have any choice. We wouldn't choose to get ill and die, if we had the choice. So illness and death are our teachers. And to the mind that can be quite depressing!
(Laughter)

Q. Yes, it all seems pointless.

Yes, that's how the mind will hear this. That it's all pointless. It hears that there's no choice and it goes, "oh shit! What's the point in carrying on!"
(Laughter)

You see, it can't hear this. That what it thinks is death, is absolute freedom. The mind sees it as death, as something to fear. That's it's way of protecting itself. It doesn't want to give up control. Its job is to go out into the world and go "I'm doing this, I'm in control, I'm king of the world!" It's like a constant mantra. The moment you wake up in the morning, it begins. "I'm doing this, I'm waking up, I'm getting out of bed, I'm brushing my teeth, I'm having breakfast, I'm going to work." And on and on. It's incessant.

This cannot be understood but it can be seen. And the simplicity of that seeing destroys all questions, because it destroys the one who asks the questions, the "me". And in fact it's already being seen. And in that seeing, choice can go on, or the story of choice, anyway. Breathing happens, and the heart beats, and thoughts come out of nowhere, and in hindsight the mind goes "I did that!" And so, thinking that it did that, it doesn't want to let go. So it's lost in this illusion.

Q. That's not to deny that there's choice, it's just that there's nobody who's choosing.

Yes, the play of choice goes on. Absolutely. I can apparently choose to clench my fist now. (Clenches fist) Undeniably, the play of choice goes on. The mind doesn't want to stay with the absolute spontaneity of what happens, because that absolute spontaneity cannot be *known*. To the mind, if something cannot be known, it's worthless, it's pointless. And actually that not knowing is absolute freedom, complete liberation, whatever you want to call it, and it's all that's ever happening.

$\sim$

Q. So is the mind just telling a story? It's not actually *doing* anything?

Ultimately the mind isn't doing anything. It has no control. These stories just *arise*. Stories about this apparent outside world, they just arise.

Q. Do you have stories?

Stories can arise. To function in the world, they appear to be necessary. There is nothing wrong with stories, that's the point. This life that we appear to live is just a wonderful play of stories. Happy stories, sad stories, but stories all the same. And a story is not serious. It's just a story. So if someone asks me my name, there is a response: "my name is Jeff". I don't go round telling people that I have no name, that I am not here, and so on.

Q. There are a lot of horrible stories. That's a sticking point.

It's very easy to hear about Oneness being the trees, the flowers, the sky, and all the beautiful stuff. It's much harder to hear that Oneness is *everything*. It's the dog poo on the ground. It's serial killers. It's the Holocaust. The mind doesn't want to hear that.

But at the same time, this isn't a cold detachment from the world. It's not a *denial* of the harsh realities of life. Nor is it a blind *acceptance* of cruelty, violence and so on. It doesn't mean that you sit back and do nothing. It doesn't mean that you *condone* the Holocaust, for example. All of this is how it may be heard. And all of this misses the point entirely.

Q. Yes, you tend to move more *towards* the pain and the suffering when awakening happens.

Exactly. Because you're not separate from any of it. There are no separate people.

And yet, there's an old man walking across the road, and you don't sit back and say to yourself "there's nobody there, nobody is walking across the road, it's all my story, it's all perfect as it is... so I don't need to do anything." That would be to take this, and use it as a philosophy, in order to justify action. That's the mind grasping again!

What I find, is that the old man is seen, and there is just *movement*, to help him across the road, and it comes from nowhere. And there's no sense that I'm doing it, there's no sense that I'm trying to be a good person. There's no sense that I'm doing it because it's the compassionate thing to do. It just does itself. And there is amazement at that. I'm helping *myself* across the road.

Q. So it happens spontaneously, and it's not the result of an agenda, or a moral code?

There's no agenda. In the absence of the separate person, there is just compassion. This is what the word "compassion" really points to: the end of separation. The word is from the Latin - it literally means "to suffer along with". To see that your suffering is not separate from my suffering. That suffering is not owned by anyone. That there is really nothing between us, apart from our stories, which are just figments of the imagination anyway.

The word "love" points to this too. And the word "non-duality".

But this compassion isn't something that you *do*. It's all there *is*. And in the seeing of this, there is just effortless action. But there's no way of knowing what action there will be. There's no way of knowing that you'll cross the road to help the old man.

Q. Presumably, you may not?

Yes. But there's no way of knowing. This cannot be used as a philosophy. This isn't another set of guidelines, telling you how to live, what to feel, how to treat others. There's enough of that in the world.

(Pause)

Of course, you may push the old man over, just for a bit of fun.
(Laughter)

I'm joking of course.

Q. For lack of a better description, when understanding takes place, or when the separate self is seen through, it seems to me that although one talks about stories arising, my experience is that energetic arisings happen more in the realm of feelings and bodily sensations. I've been through a lot of health concerns in the last few months, with apparent realities, although when they're looked at medically not much is seen. But the experience is first this, then that, then this. There's an experience of an energetic momentum. Stories aren't arising on the level

of story anymore, it's stories arising on the level of feelings. The residues of self-concern that remain, they're on the level of bodily concern. When understanding takes place, is there a process where the bodily organism settles in with this? Is that your experience, or is that just another conceptual way of looking at it?

There are no rules.

Q. In my manifestation the idea of being a separate person has been around for a long time. There seems to be an accumulation of residue.

There is no residue.

Q. Is there only one manifestation?

Yes, and it appears in the form of many separate manifestations. That's the mystery of it. It's a constant wonder.

Q. So this so-called energetic manifestation is taking place... and that's all there is to it?

Yes, and even *that* is just another story.

Q. *In* that?

In that, yes. It's amazing.

Q. But it's not something you can do anything about?

It's all given. Already. It's all given. But we can't see it because we're looking for it.

Nothing needs to be done. It doesn't ask anything of you, at all. It's absolutely unconditional.

We're like newborn babies. That's what we are.

Q. Because to want part of the manifestation to leave, that would be a wanting, and that's a condition?

Yes, that would be to put a condition on the unconditional.

You see, it's happening now. It's staring you in the face.

Q. Does putting conditions on it stop you from seeing it?

Absolutely not. Conditions are allowed to arise in this. Even the idea of conditions is allowed to arise in this! The mind might hear this and go "right, I need to get rid of conditions", and that's just another goal. So the mind is always buying itself time. It loves the future, it wants a future, in order to keep itself alive. It will do anything to get a future! *(Laughter)*

The idea of some sort of block to this is just an idea happening now.

This is happening, and in this arises the idea that I'm a person. It's just an idea, and that's all it has ever been. Your entire life, from the very beginning it was only an idea. Me, me, me. I, I, I. And everything was built upon that.

And that can become very heavy. We become like snails with heavy shells.
(Laughter)

That was good, wasn't it? I'll write that one down!
(Laughter)

Q. So freedom is like being a slug?
(Laughter)

Yes, that's today's take-home message. Freedom is like being a slug!

~

Q. I find that listening to this, there is a sense that I should just sit back and watch the show. If the show is just watched, and just seen as a show, then it's all okay.

And yet it's not a cold detachment from the show. You are the show. You are not separate from the show. It's not that you sit back and watch it.

Q. Yes, I get that.

You are the show, and the show is you. It's all fully yourself... and yet it's got nothing to do with you. Totally personal, completely impersonal. To the mind, that's an absolute paradox. Actually there is no paradox at all.

(Pause)

Q1. Look, it's snowing!

(Everyone looks outside at the falling snow)

Q2. No, it's just thoughts arising!
(Laughter)

Q3. Do thoughts ever descend?
(Laughter)

You see, everything's just weather. It comes and goes. The body. Thoughts, feelings. Seeking.

Q4. And nobody knows, not even the weather men!
(Laughter)

Especially the weather men!

Q. Self-consciousness seems to be a block.

There's no blocks to this.

Q. Ageing seems to be another block.

A ninety year-old lady called me the other day. She sees this so clearly. Finally she has seen that everything is a story. She was giggling on the phone. Roaring with laughter. This has nothing to do with age.
(Laughter)

Q. That's just another excuse from the mind, isn't it?

Yes. I'm too old, I'm too ignorant, I'm too this, I'm too that. Just an excuse.

Q. Or that I'm falling apart.

Yes. Or my past has been too heavy. Any excuse.

Q. Yes, I feel a lot of that.

And that's what the mind *has* to do. It *has* to resist this. It's terrified.

And yet it's absolutely innocent, and it's not the enemy. It's just terrified of letting go, because it doesn't know any better.

Q. Yes, that's what seems to happen. It's fine for a while and then the fear comes up.

Yes. You know, this has nothing to do with age, with physical health, with intelligence, with anything. I know a guy who's on morphine, in constant pain, and he says that in the midst of the most intense pain, it's seen that there is nobody there. There's nobody there who's in pain. And in that, the pain is released. It's allowed to be itself. To be fully painful.

So the pain is fully there, and it's allowed, by no one, to be as it is, and arise and dissolve of its own accord, and yet it's seen so clearly that the pain is not there at all. It's just not there.

The mind hasn't a hope of understanding this. This has

nothing to do with age, nothing to do with physical health. There are no blocks to this, and the fear is just a tactic the mind uses to *try* and block it.

Q. Why would someone like that, who sees this so clearly, come to these meetings?

Friendship.

Q. It's just meeting friends.

Yes. Oneness resonating with itself. There's a joy in that. It seems to delight in meeting itself.

Q. When there is Oneness, what happens to the mind?

Well, when we say "mind", we just mean thought. Presently arising thought, that's all there is. There's no solid entity there called "mind". It's a figure of speech. So in that sense, nothing happens to the mind. In another sense, thought is liberated. It's just seen that it's not personal, and so the suffering goes out of it.

Q. I meant, what happens to speech, and working things out?

Oh, it's astonishing. Effortlessly, things get done. As they do already. Already, nobody wakes up in the morning, nobody gets out of bed, nobody brushes their teeth. Already, it's doing itself. Nobody goes to the shops. Nobody goes to work.
(Laughter)

So already there is this effortlessness, right at the heart of life. And in the absence of seeking, everything falls back into its natural rhythm. And don't ask me how!

Q. It's a release, isn't it?

It's the absolute release. You *find* yourself in a shop, you *find* yourself at work, you *find* yourself brushing your teeth. It's a constant discovery. I *find* myself here today, doing this. Apparently!
(Laughter)

And yet even to say that I find myself doing this is a lie. All I find is this, doing itself. I am nowhere to be found. I am just a story.

This is a constant wonder. And there are no more questions. "Who's doing this? Am I doing this? Who's in charge? Where does it all come from?" All of that falls away. There is just a resting with what is. It's a kind of trust. But it's not a trust that you're *doing*.

And all of this isn't just an intellectual understanding. It's what it actually feels like. It *feels* effortless. It *feels* like it's doing itself. Any yet nobody feels any of this. It is as it is, and that's the end of it.

And yet, if you ask me a question, I'll tell you a very ordinary story.

Part Two

Q. Jeff, do you have thoughts and feelings?
(Laughter)

No, I'm beyond thoughts and feelings! I've transcended this world!
(Laughter)

Q. It's just that, if you do, they're not here and now.

Oh, they absolutely are.

Q. Well, the story seems to be that there is an awareness in which this character arises. And there is only that one awareness. And in that awareness, *your* thoughts and feelings aren't here. There's the external appearance of you, but not your thoughts and feelings.

Oh, that's the absolute mystery of this! There is only Oneness, but in Oneness, the personal appears. The character appears. There appears to be this character called Jeff, and this character called, say, Bob. And in the story, Jeff has thoughts and feelings, and Bob has thoughts and feelings, and there can appear to be a relationship between these two illusory entities. That's the story. That's the dream of individuality.

But when the separate individual falls away, it simply doesn't matter anymore what arises. What we call "Jeff" arises and dissolves in this. "Bob" arises and dissolves in this. Thoughts and feelings arise and dissolve in this. We could tell the story that those thoughts and feelings *belong* to Jeff. But really they are liberated. They are not owned by anyone. They arise and dissolve in absolute freedom. Still, we can tell the story "Jeff has thoughts and feelings". But really, it ceases to matter whether or not Jeff is there at all, let alone whether or not he has thoughts and feelings.

Q. It seems to me that the idea that you have thoughts and feelings, and that I have thoughts and feelings, and that they don't know about each other, is separation.

Yes, that's the *game*. That's the play of apparent characters. It doesn't need to be rejected or denied. Of course, in reality, Jeff doesn't do anything. Jeff is just a story.

Jeff cannot *have* thoughts and feelings. Jeff *is* thoughts and feelings, and everything else that arises.

Q. Nor can Bob.

Yes. Jeff and Bob are just appearances in the One reality, in this. Over here, Jeff is just a story arising. And Bob is just a story arising. And so Jeff and Bob, and their apparent relationships, play themselves itself out in this. Jeff and Bob arise in the absolute intimacy that the separate characters Jeff and Bob could never see, touch, smell, hear or taste. And yet, the intimacy is all there is. It's all that's being seen, touched, tasted…

Q. My only experience has been from *this* point, seeing this world. So as far as I'm concerned, you don't even

exist. You are me, telling me to wake up. Is that correct? How can Oneness see the world from lots of different places?

That question arises for an individual who thinks that they are separate. All these questions do. It's the individual, who believes they're separate, doing the asking. When the individual falls away, the questions die too.

Q. But something still has to perceive, right? Why does it use my eyes and not your eyes?

Because I'm special!
(Laughter)

No, I'm joking. You're all special!
(Laughter)

You see, Oneness is looking through *these* eyes and *those* eyes, and *those* eyes, and hearing through *these* ears, and *those* ears, and *those* ears. Oneness delights in that. It doesn't prefer *these* ears to *those* ears. It doesn't distinguish between *this* person and *that* person. It doesn't know anything about the separation thing. It's absolute equality. So *this* seeing is equal to *that* seeing, and *this* hearing is equal to *that* hearing and so on. Oneness doesn't "choose" to use your eyes instead of my eyes.

Q. But imagine there's a delusion here, and the delusion falls away. There's still consciousness at my co-ordinates.

And that question arises for a "me".

Q. So who's inside looking out?

There's *nothing* inside looking out. There's no inside and outside. That's the illusion that falls away. And when it falls away it's seen in utter clarity that there's just *this*, and really *this* has no name. You can't even really call it *this*.

You know, I love it when people look at me and think there's somebody here. What a wonderful game it is to play at being Jeff, and know that there is only Being, and no Jeff separate from Being.

Q. So it's Oneness looking through...?

Oh, the moment we talk about it we're back into our theories. Into the story. It's too obvious to talk about. Too simple. It cannot be captured by any theory.

To the individual, it all seems to be a paradox. If there is only Oneness, why does it appear as though I'm here and you're there? But that's the individual asking. When the individual falls away, that question becomes meaningless.

The paradox is resolved in the falling away of the paradox. And then it's seen: the paradox was never there. It was just a game the mind was playing, trying to keep itself alive. All questions are burnt up by the clarity.

Q. To me, the idea of seeing, not from a personal perspective, but in some other way, is completely meaningless. It's like saying that I see the front and back of something

at the same time. It doesn't mean anything to me at all. (Pause) I just thought I'd tell you that!
(Laughter)

Oh, it doesn't mean anything to me either!
(Laughter)

I never understood this. I never believed it. I couldn't believe it if I tried. It's not about understanding or belief.

～

Q1. It's like, if Oneness is Shakespeare, and he's writing the parts for everyone in his play, it doesn't mean that the people in the play understand the whole of the play, from where Shakespeare is looking. So really you are a character in his play. Does that help anyone?
(Laughter)

Q2. You lost me about five minutes ago!

～

Q. The thing is, if you're angry, I can feel it. Doesn't that imply separation?

In Oneness there appears to be separation. There appear to be separate bodies. Undeniably so.

And that's it. That's the mystery. There's no need to make a single movement away from that. It's nothing arising as everything. The appearance of emptiness as form. And it's constantly happening. In any situation, it's still the mystery happening. Sitting on the toilet, making a cup of tea, climbing Mount Everest, it's still the mystery, still the miracle.

Really, I cannot feel "your" anger. Because your anger isn't yours. My anger isn't mine. There is no "mine" and "yours". Just the isness. Just what is. Just the energy of it. And the mind comes in and calls it "yours" or "mine", and weaves a tale around that. What you are experiencing, what you did to me, what I'll do to you, and so on. That's the *story* of anger. That's the story of separation.

In reality, there's just anger arising, and it's already arising for no one. It's arising in emptiness. And in the absence of the person trying to manipulate it, it just burns up, in its own time.

And, what's more astonishing: it's seen that anger isn't really anger at all. Really, it has no name. It's just energy. And it's fully there and it's not there. This is a place the mind could never, ever go. The mind has no hope of understanding this.

It's an astonishing revelation. And yet, when seen, it's as obvious as breathing. Tony Parsons calls it the *Open Secret*.

Q. The mind seems to want it to not be a mystery. So there's that search to understand the mystery, rather than just be with it. But it's a mystery, and that's it.

Yes, the mind doesn't want to stay with the mystery. It can't. Well, it can stay with it for a few seconds. And then comes the "yeah, but...."

But there's no condemnation of that here. It all just plays itself out. If we had the choice, we'd choose for it to stop now.

Q. You talk about the mind sometimes, and it makes it sound like a solid thing.

When I say "mind", I just mean thought. Presently-arising thought. And of course, the moment you say it, it sounds like it's solid, it sounds like it's real, it sounds like it has some sort of permanence. Undeniably, there is something going on though. *Mind, thought, stories, knowledge, ideas.* Call it what you will. To say "there is no mind" is only half the story.

The point is, there will appear to be a mind until it's seen in clarity that there is no mind, just presently arising thought. Until then, there appears to be a solid entity there, and there appears to be mesmerisation with the thought story. When it's all seen through, there is no possibility of mesmerisation because there is nobody there to be mesmerised, and no mind to mesmerise. There is only what's happening, and no way of knowing it. In that, the mind is destroyed, and thought is released to arise and dissolve naturally. Thought falls back into its natural rhythm. It becomes what it always was: a useful tool, and nothing more. It no longer has any power. It never did, actually.

Q. Thoughts *seem* to have tremendous power though.

Yes, they can have a momentum. The same thoughts *seem*

to arise over and over again. They seem to have a pattern to them.

And actually, the *seeming* is the identity. The appearance of a pattern is the identity. Really there is no pattern. Thoughts are always new, always fresh. Because they are not yours. But they seem to be linked up in some way, and that linking is the personal identity. The sense of continuity is the identity.

Q. You say they seem fresh, and I suppose in reality they are, but when they've been thought so many times, they seem to have more energy to them. Painful thoughts can be very powerful.

A painful thought is a thought that you don't want to be there.

Q. So say, there's a thought "nobody likes me". You're saying that the thought isn't painful, but the pain is in the rejection of the thought, the not allowing of the thought. The thought that it's not okay.

Yes, and at the root of it all, there's the idea that this thought has something to do with a personal "me".

Q. Yes. They're rejecting *me*.

Which implies there's a me here to reject! Actually when it's seen that there is no entity here, that thought no longer has any power. And yet it's allowed to arise, if it arises, because there's no longer anybody there fighting it. Any thought is allowed to arise, and do its little dance, and dissolve of its own accord, as everything does.

Q. But the thought "nobody likes me" can actually manifest as being somebody who does get rejected.

Of course.

Q. That's how it works, isn't it?

Yes.

Q. And the thought is just fresh in the moment, but it seems like it's very real.

It's in the *seeming*, you see.

Q. Yes, it *seems* real. So at any moment there's an opportunity to see clearly that it's just this, it's just that.

Yes, and in that, the thought is still allowed to arise. This isn't a rejection of thought. It's amazing. Any thought is allowed to arise. And thoughts that you once thought were the most terrible thoughts of all, they are still allowed to arise. And it can be seen: "Oh, it's just a thought!"

You see, we make thoughts into the enemy.

Q. We could say that the pain is making it real.

And at the root of that, is the feeling of being separate.

Q. Which comes from the thought of being separate?

They are one and the same.

Q. Doesn't the thought create the feeling?

There is no separation between mind and body. The thought *is* the feeling. The feeling *is* the thought. They don't create each other. They *are* each other. Different perspectives, that's all.

Q. So what is the feeling of separation?

Not being at home. Not being complete. At the root of all suffering is the idea that you are separate from what's happening.

So, take physical pain. There's pain arising, and the mind has already called it pain. *Me and my pain. I have pain. It's my pain. What can I do with my pain?* To the mind, the pain shouldn't be there. That's the suffering.

Actually, what's happening cannot be known.

Q. So, it seems like there's pain. But what you're saying is that there isn't pain. It's just a sensation, and it's being called pain, but it's not pain. Is that what you're saying?

It not anything. It is what it is, and it cannot be known. You could call it energy, but even to do that is to put a box around it, to make it solid.

Q. It can't be known?

It's just aliveness. Aliveness cannot be known. It cannot

be captured by thought, a dead thing. And aliveness is not separate from anything else. Really there's no pain energy separate from any other energy. But the mind calls it pain, puts a boundary there, makes it into a thing. The mind kills it. So it becomes "me and my pain". "I am person experiencing pain. I don't want to be experiencing pain." That's the suffering.

Without the story of pain, without the suffering, you cannot know pain as pain. You cannot experience pain as pain. You experience what you know. So in that not knowing, you cannot experience pain, because you are no longer separate from pain.

And that doesn't mean it doesn't hurt! But the hurting isn't a problem. And what happens, is that it all becomes very *interesting*. Pain, or what we call pain, becomes very interesting. It's very alive. In the middle of the most intense pain, there is this aliveness, this childlike wonder at the world. And in that aliveness, the pain burns up.

So, we could say that the pain is there, but it isn't there. Superficially, the pain is there, but right at the heart of the pain, there is no pain. Remember Jesus on the cross. Right at the heart of the most intense physical suffering known to man, God was there. Eternal Life, right at the heart of pain. Again, the mind has no hope of understanding this. But it *is*, whether we understand it or not.

Q. Can this seeing happen *through* pain?

Pain teaches us that we have no control. We wouldn't choose to be in pain, if we had the choice. But inevitably, we will experience pain during our lifetime. It's out of our hands. It just happens. As long as there is this physical form, pain is possible. The suffering is in the not wanting the pain to be there. When there is no longer anyone doing that, the pain is liberated.

And yet, resistance to pain can still arise. But it is seen that it's just thoughts. "I don't want the pain to be there." Just thoughts. And thoughts are not a problem when it's seen that they have no power at all.

You know, pain doesn't ask anything of us. It doesn't want to be manipulated. It doesn't want to be grasped or controlled. It just wants to live. It wants to arise and dissolve of its own accord. That's what everything wants. Just to be allowed to be itself. Pain just wants to be pain. Sadness just wants to be sadness. Anger just wants to be anger.

Pain doesn't need us. And when that is seen, pain is released. It's released to be itself. So pain can be fully painful. It can be what it is. Which it already is! So the individual who thinks they are separate from pain, *that's* the suffering. The suffering *is* the individual. So everything we do to try and end our pain just fuels the suffering, fuels the sense of being a victim. Pain was never yours in the first place.

So pain is already arising in freedom. We search for freedom from pain, and that's the suffering. The freedom was always at the centre of the pain, right at its core. The freedom is in the seeing that the pain is already happening for no one. It's just arising in emptiness, and dancing, and being painful. That's it's job. We don't want the pain to be painful. That's the suffering.

The mind will only ever hear paradox here. The pain can be fully painful, and not be a problem. You know, very young children see this. They fall over and scrape their knee, and it hurts for a moment, and then they're up and running around and their attention has been captured by something else. There's a lightness to it. There isn't that desperation for an identity. The "poor me, why did it have to happen to me", that's the suffering you see.

So really, pain is just God in disguise, telling us to wake up and see this.

Q. So you're saying that the ownership of pain doesn't happen, when this is seen?

Ownership is only a thought. "It's mine" – just a thought. And those thoughts are still allowed to arise. Everything is allowed to arise. This is what all those spiritual teachers are talking about when they tell us to surrender, or allow what's happening, or become more present. They have a sense of this. But really all there is, is the allowing. All there is, is the presence. All there is, is a constant surrendering. This is already what's happening. What's happening now is already being allowed. And nobody is doing it. Nobody is sitting in this room, allowing all of this to happen. That would be a full time job!

And I say this is already being allowed, because it's

happening. It's in the simplicity of the *happening,* that's where the miracle is. And that destroys all spiritual seeking, or any type of seeking for that matter. That's the end of it.

∿

Q. So there's no such thing as a thinker?

There appears to be!
(Laughter)

Q. But you can choose to think.

Can you?

Q. I know what you're saying. I've seen it both ways.

And actually the "both ways" are reflections of each other. Really, there's no separation. It's just the appearance of choice, the appearance of the thinker.

Q. Or is it just the identification? You can say there is just pure thinking. And the great It is doing it, God is doing it, the Divine is doing it, or whatever. That would be a more accurate identification, rather than saying that there is an "I" apart from the thinking.

Yes, but that cannot be known. It cannot be understood intellectually that God is doing it. Of course, you could tell yourself "God is doing it, God is doing it", but really that changes nothing. You are just left with an intellectual understanding, just concepts and nothing more. This is beyond all of that.

This is the vast Unknown. And in the vast Unknown arises the idea of choice. The idea that I'm thinking, the idea of a thinker of thoughts. For example, there could be the idea that you chose to come here today. And the mind goes "yes, of course I did it." But that could only ever be a story, arising in this, the vast Unknown. The story happens *in* this. The story isn't at war with this, it happens *in* this. The story of apparent choice.

Q. Yes, I understand that.

It leaves you here. The story is always told in hindsight.

Q. So it doesn't really matter what the description is. Whether God's doing it, or you're doing it. It's when it becomes wordless, that it's happening. I get it.

Yes, then there's no need for words.

Q. But we use words to communicate.

Yes. And that's all that's happening here. Using words to point to that which could never be spoken of. We have to use words. But it's never about the words. And there's nothing wrong with words.

Q. Oh, they're good fun! *(Giggles)*
(Laughter)

Q. You can tell wonderful stories. Have wonderful visions.

Q. If there is just awareness, is there anything left in deep sleep?

In deep sleep there's nothing. And nobody there to know that.

You see, this is how unreal this dream world is. At night you go to sleep, and it all falls away. And you wake up in the morning, and it comes back for a while. It's all so evanescent. And actually there is no continuity there at all, there is no solid "self" that experiences all of this. It's the self that comes and goes upon waking and sleeping.

Why are we so afraid of death, then? Every morning we are born again, every night we get to die! Every time we go to sleep, we are tasting death. It's like God giving us practice! And yet we fear death because we think it's different from sleep. But what is sleep but the end of seeking? What is death but eternal rest, the end of suffering?

Of course, we fear death because it's the end of the self, the end of continuity. But as we just said, there is no such thing. And so when all of that falls away, there's no sleeping and waking at all, and no death, because there's no entity here who falls asleep and wakes up and dies. There is only what's happening. Only this and nothing more. You could call it constant awakeness, constant aliveness. It's untouched by death.

Q. Infinite intelligence must be there all the time.

All the time. Even in deep, dreamless sleep, Oneness is there. All the spiritual teachings point to this in the end. They often speak of this world as a dream world. It's essentially unreal. It's simply not there in deep dreamless sleep. And yet, this infinite intelligence, completely beyond the mind, continues to function, constantly.

There is essentially no difference between dreaming and waking life. It's just that when we're awake, we think we have choice.

Q. Apparently the Aborigines, when they were first introduced to our way of life, were very puzzled. They were brought up to believe that their dream life was real, and their waking life was a dream. So they had a lot of trouble getting their head round our understanding.

Yes, it's all in the perspective.

And the wonderful thing about dreams is that they are so light. So evanescent.

Q. They're like cartoons.

Yes, and anything can happen in cartoons. There can be happy scenes and sad scenes. A bad dream, a good dream, they are both still just dreams.

Q. So Oneness remains in deep sleep?

And there's nobody there to know that.

Q. I've heard it said that when you awaken, you can watch yourself sleep.

Oh, there's all these ideas about what will happen when you awaken. Firstly, "you" cannot awaken! Secondly, any experience is just another experience. That's not what we're talking about here.

Q. In Vedanta, they talk about you being there when you're asleep.

When this was first seen, I experienced a lot of lucid dreaming. But you know, it just didn't matter anymore! It didn't matter what arose! Whether it was lucid dreaming or lying in bed at night watching the stars. Whatever you can experience, it's still part of the dream. It's the dream character lucid dreaming! It's the dream character who experiences bliss! For there to be any experience, there must still be an experiencer. When the experiencer falls away, then there is total equanimity with whatever arises, whether it's lucid dreaming or watching the stars or eating fish and chips or whatever.

Anything you think you'll experience when you awaken, that's still part of the dream. It's still an *idea*. What falls away when this is seen, is the desire for any *particular* experience. For anything other than what's happening. What's happening is always enough. In that, the seeking of the mind burns up.

Q. I have real tangible fear. It's been growing throughout

this afternoon. It's something to do with not being able to understand all of this.

It's the mind feeling threatened.

Q. It's scary.

Yes, but the fear is groundless. There is just the fear. There's nothing to be afraid *of.* That's the story the mind is using to keep itself going. It says there's something to fear. There's nothing to fear. Literally. There's just the fear, with no object.

And actually fear is quite exciting. It's an opening up. The fear is the final tactic the mind uses to keep itself going. It's a tricky little bugger, the mind.
(Laughter)

Q. It can be like standing in a strong wind. Exhilaration. Energy moving.

It's very alive. It's more alive than any concept about enlightenment. Because it's happening. It's undeniably there. It's the mind feeling threatened. But there's nothing to fear. You know, I was once terrified of this. Terrified.

Q. Wayne Liquorman says the ego comes out and says "What are you doing? You're nothing without me!"
(Laughter)

Yes, that's the beauty of this. The "nothing" terrifies the mind. But it's not an empty nothing. It's a very full, alive nothing – a no-thing that's vast enough to be filled with

173

whatever's happening. Filled with sights and sounds and smells, filled with anything that presents itself. And that's all there is, and it's a constant wonder.

Q. My mind stays alive by not wanting things to be the way they are. By not liking the way I am.

The mind is innocent. It doesn't know. If it knew what it was doing, it wouldn't do it. That's why Jesus said "Forgive them father, for they know not what they do." The mind hasn't a clue.

Q. It's very destructive.

Actually it's not. The mind has no power. Presence cannot be destroyed. It's like what the scientists say: Energy cannot be created or destroyed, it can only be converted from one form into another.

All the mind can do is tell its stories. It cannot create or destroy a damn thing.

Q. Can nothing be created through thought?

Well, thought likes to take credit for everything. "I made this. I did this". Actually it's being done. It's Oneness working its magic through you, you could say.

Q. Through the use of the imagination?

What we are talking about is the source of *all* creativity. It's the absolute paradox. In the absence of you, that's where the magic happens. That's the Source. The source of all creativity. And it appears to manifest through you. Something coming out of nothing. The only miracle.

Q. So is there no such thing as an inspired idea?

All ideas are inspired!

Q. And some thoughts appear to be creative, and some appear to be counter-productive let us say. And whilst thought is still doing its thing, it makes sense to choose thoughts that make me feel better, as opposed to thoughts that make me feel miserable!
(Laughter)

Oh, stay with what works for you, absolutely. Reject anything that doesn't. You could say that as long as you believe that you have a choice, you appear to have a choice! When it's seen that there's no choice, there's no choice, and it all unfolds effortlessly.

Q. Yes, if you're going to be thinking anyway, then it makes sense to me to think something positive. My favourite thoughts are ones that say that God is divine, and he's everywhere, and so on. Then, what happens, is that my mind begins to settle, and this organism feels more peaceful, and the quiet spaces are more likely to arise.

And actually those quiet spaces don't *arise* at all. All there is, is a quiet space that allows the world to unfold. Including the happiness and the sadness. The happy thoughts and the sad thoughts. Those all play themselves out, in this space. Call it God, call it Spirit, call it Oneness.

But absolutely, none of your concepts, your theories, your understanding need to be rejected. That's the beauty of this message. It's unconditional love. It allows everything to have its place. It allows religions. It allows belief systems. It allows every concept known to man. It allows them all to be there. It allows life as it already is.

Q. Yes, I understand that.

It's already complete. In every moment, it's complete. To the person looking for completion, it's never complete. But the cosmic joke, is that even *that* is part of the completion!

Q. What is death?

There is no death. There is no entity here who was born. There is nothing here that's separate from life. Just an openness in which the story of the individual arises, and that openness is not separate from anything that arises. So on death, all that falls away is a story. But the story wasn't real in the first place. It's just a story.

Now, to the mind that's terrifying. The loss of the story, the loss of the known, the loss of control. So really, death is a plunge into the Unknown, which is where you always are. It's where you are now.

Q. Death has never been something I was afraid of. There is a knowing that there is no death.

There's no death because *this* cannot die.

There is only aliveness. Even a moment before what we call death, there is still only aliveness. And in that aliveness, yes, there can be pain. And then, upon what we call death, there's nobody there to know it. It's a plunge into the Unknown. And that's all that's happening anyway. There's nothing to fear.

And really what we're talking about today is that we don't have to wait until physical death to see this. Die before you die, and then there is no death. And in that death, there is only absolute aliveness. What's happening now, this is death. There's nothing to fear here!

We see other people die. We see their body functioning one minute, and then ceasing to function the next and we say "that's going to happen to me one day".

Q. It's the fear of the loss of identity.

Yes.

Q. That's what we cling to.

And that identity can be seen through now. And then there's no fear. And then there's no death.

A few years ago our cat got very ill, and we had to have her put down. I was holding her whilst the vet put the needle into her. She was obviously in pain. But there was no death for her. The concept of death meant nothing to her. For her, there was just what was happening. Pain, and then the prick of a needle, and then maybe a warm sensation in her body. But no idea that she was about to die. No attachment to a "me". No clinging to the past. No regrets.

We fear death because we know it. We have an idea of what it is. That's the fear.

Q. When my husband died, six years ago, there was just love. There was no pain, no sadness, there was just... love.

It's all there is.

(Long silence)

DIALOGUE FOUR

Abundance

*When you really understand that
you are what you see and know,
you don't run around the countryside thinking,
"I am all this!"*

There is simply all this.

Alan Watts

Part One

The secret of spiritual awakening is staring us in the face, but we cannot see it, because we are looking for it. It's always happening, but we're so lost in the *seeking* game, in the search for something *more* than what's presently happening, that it eludes us, perhaps for a lifetime.

What we're talking about today is the possibility that you were *never* separate from life, from this, from what you seek. There has only ever been Oneness. And it's happening now. Wherever you are, not just in this room! And it doesn't take a future to see this. This isn't something that you will see at the end of a long spiritual path. This isn't something for you to "get". It's already all there is. Well, of course it is, Oneness must be all there is! It wouldn't be Oneness otherwise!

This isn't about giving up anything. It's not about giving up spiritual practices. It's not about giving up the search. That just becomes another goal, doesn't it? The giving up? If it were that easy to give up the search, we'd have done it by now. If we were choosing to seek, choosing to suffer, we wouldn't choose to seek and suffer! The point is, you are not doing any of this. You are not doing the seeking, you are not doing the suffering. Already – and this is the secret at the heart of all religions and spiritual teachings – life lives itself. *Not my will, but Thy will be done.* Already, Oneness is doing this, and you are just a character in a divine movie. Call it Oneness, call it God, call it Spirit, call it Energy, or call it nothing at all, it's that which allows everything to be. And it's not separate from everything that is. And it's not separate from what you are.

And this can be seen right now: breathing is happening and you're not doing it. The heart is beating and you're not doing it. Sounds in the room are happening and you aren't doing the hearing. That's the mind coming in and grasping: "I'm doing it! I'm hearing! I'm seeing! Me, me, me!" So there's always this illusion of "me" at the centre of my life. And actually, on closer inspection, it's just not there. If you've ever meditated, you'll have a sense of this. On closer inspection, all you can find is presently-arising thoughts, presently-arising sounds, smells, feelings. But nobody there who is doing all of this. It's all a spontaneous play, with nobody in control. All an effortless happening, an energetic dance, a wonderfully evanescent play of light and sound, not appearing to a *someone*, but happening for *no one*.

And Oneness takes a billion different forms. Right now, it's taking the form of a bunch of people in a room, listening to someone else talk. This is the dream, this is the story, that there are some people in a room listening to someone else talk! Actually, all that's happening, is Oneness. And when this is seen with absolute clarity, the whole search for something *more* dies. There's no use for it anymore. Because what is, is seen to be all there is. There's simply no possibility of anything else. And in fact it was always the seeking that made this into a problem. It was the search for the extraordinary that kept this ordinary. Once that search falls away, this is seen to be quite extraordinary. And yet, it's so utterly ordinary. And this is shocking to the mind. The mind goes "it can't be this, this is too ordinary!" This destroys all of the mind's ideas about awakening.

But you see, the miracle was always here, right here, in the ordinary things. It's always been right here.

(A baby cries in the background)

It's in the hearing of a baby crying. But we want so much more than that. To the mind, it's *just* a baby crying. It's all so ordinary. It's all so... known. Actually, this is Oneness, constantly presenting itself. In the form of a baby crying, in breathing, in the feeling of your bum on the chair. And the separate person, the seeker, could never find this. Because actually the seeker, the "me", the person who wants this, is just a thought! Just a story. A story arising in this.

You know, life asks nothing of you. That's the gift of it. It just presents itself, in this form now. And then in this form. And this. And there's no way of knowing what will happen next! We're always right at the heart of it, the Unknown, the Unborn, the Undying.

This message can be quite challenging to a mind that wants to hold on to its beliefs, to a mind that wants something to do. But this message won't give the mind anything to do. But we're also not saying that we should give up any of our doing. The point is, you have no choice. Actually, the secret is that the doing is already happening. It's already doing itself. This is a play of Oneness, and you're not in control of it. So whether you find yourself sitting here, or walking through a park, or sitting down to meditate or self-enquire, you are not doing it. Already, Oneness is playing this game, and you are just a thought arising presently. Already, this is being done. What needs to be done, is being done. *Not my will, but Thy will.* Oneness is already complete, and anything you do or don't do cannot add to, or take away from, that completion.

So, right now, there's the heart beating. Thoughts arising, perhaps. Sounds happening. You know, we're just newborn babies. That's all we are. That's all we ever were.

(Baby cries in the background)

Wow, right on cue!
(Laughter)

You know, this is all choreographed! I'm paying him, you know!
(Laughter)

It's constant. The beauty of this, is that is cannot be had by you. But it cannot be lost, either. Anything that you can get, you can lose. This cannot be had, so it cannot be lost. It can't be grasped. But the beauty of this unconditional love, is that it even allows the grasping to go on, for as long as it goes on, until it doesn't anymore. And the grasping and seeking, they play themselves out, and eventually the mind just exhausts itself, and comes to rest. And it is seen in absolute clarity: *this is it.* Not just as an intellectual understanding, but as a clear and obvious seeing.

Yes, the mystery of the Universe is staring you in the face. It always has been. And you can't lose it. You can't have it either. But you can't lose it. It's all there is. And you're not separate from it. So when you wake up in the morning, there's just Oneness. When you brush your teeth, there's Oneness. When you make breakfast, there's Oneness.

When you go to work, there's Oneness. And you come back home, and you go to bed, and Oneness is still all there is. It's there even in deep dreamless sleep. It's constant.

But this isn't about enlightened *people*, or awakened *people*. Anyone who claims to be an enlightened *person*, or an awakened *person*, is still lost in this dream of separation, the illusion of individuality. The *person* is just a story, part of the dream. And whether the person is awakened or not, that's still part of the dream. An awakened dream character is still just a dream character.

When the illusion of individuality falls away, there's no way of knowing who or what you are. Anyone who claims to be awakened still knows something, they know that they are awakened! They are still rich. Jesus said that it's easier for a camel to pass through the eye of a needle, than it is for a rich man to enter the Kingdom of Heaven. Yes, this is absolute poverty. But in that poverty, oh, everything is given. Freely. This is absolute abundance, and it's nothing like you ever thought it would be.

Today, we are using words to point to the obvious. There's no prescriptions here, there's no methods. Just descriptions of what is already the case. And it's not about me passing something onto you. This is simply a sharing, in friendship, from Oneness to Oneness. And it's not about the words at all. The words are pointing to something that's totally beyond words. The message is in the energy, the aliveness of it. It's a resonance that cannot be understood, and yet it's all that's happening here. So, let's play. What else is there to do!

~

Q. Since I last saw you, it's noticeable that there's a lot of silence. It's like, I'm talking now, but it doesn't feel like there's anyone talking.

That's because there isn't!

Q. It's become very apparent. There's just a lot of silence. And then, it speaks. I'm a teacher, and I prepared my classes yesterday, and I got in front of the children, and it just spoke. It was nothing like I'd prepared. It feels very empty. There's talking happening now, but I don't know how it's happening.

Oh, you're not supposed to know! We're so used to being in control. Thinking we're in control, anyway. It's a very strange thing to realise that you're not, and it's already doing itself. Effortlessly.

And actually the emptiness you talk about is really quite full. Really, there is no emptiness separate from what is happening. The emptiness is filled up by everything. This is exactly what's pointed at in the Buddhist Heart Sutra: "Form is not other than emptiness. Emptiness is not other than form." The emptiness is the talking, the breathing, the living. It's not that the emptiness is in the background, and life happens in the foreground. Actually, what happens is that the emptiness collapses into everything that happens. That's the true meaning of nonduality.

You know, I never talk about stages, but a common story is that there is a stage before the nondual realisation, where there is a residing as the emptiness, or the witness. That certainly seemed to be true over here, a while back. But even there, there is still a very subtle separation between the witness and everything that is witnessed. When the witness collapses into everything that's witnessed, it's all over. And you cannot really call that a stage, because it's the end of all stages. It's a collapse back into a very ordinary life.

Before enlightenment, chop wood and carry water. After enlightenment, chop wood and carry water. The chopping and carrying go on. A very ordinary life is lived. But it's seen in clarity that there's simply nobody living that life. The chopping wood and carrying water are done, but now they are done by nobody. And yet, if someone asks "are you chopping wood and carrying water?", there may be the very ordinary response "Yes, yes I am."

Q. I don't know how it happened. It just happened.

Yes, and there's no way you could have done it. You cannot bring about your own absence.

Q. And yet I can talk normally. It's like, everything's the same, but it doesn't feel like I'm here. But at the same time, I'm here.

Oh, it's the absolute paradox of nonduality. The moment you talk or think about it, it appears to be a paradox. Something arising out of nothing. Out of the emptiness, a very personal life seems to arise. Out of nothing, everything happens, and it's got nothing to do with you, and everything to do with you. And there's still a name, and apparent form, and yet nobody's doing it. And the moment you make a movement to try and understand that, there will only be confusion.

It cannot be known. The absolute simplicity of this cannot be known. It's the absolute mystery.

~

Q. There's a feeling of trusting it, isn't there? Of just letting it be, of not trying to understand it. But sometimes the individual comes back in, and tries to take control of the situation.

Yes, the mind comes back in, to try and fill the emptiness, to try and take back control. It gets very threatened by this. It's used to being in control, and so it can come back with a vengeance! But once this starts to unravel, it has a momentum of its own, and the mind has no chance. Once the mind's tricks begin to be seen through, it's a death sentence for the mind!

The mind going out and coming back in, you know it just starts to exhaust itself. The poor old mind doesn't really know what it's doing. It's innocent.

Q. It seems to know that something's going on. It doesn't feel comfortable making long term plans anymore.

Yes, when the futility of making plans is seen, perhaps there won't be any making of plans for a while! And then making of plans can come back. They are just plans, after all. Over here, there were no plans for a while. And then plans came back in. But even when plans are made, there is a knowing that the best laid plans often go astray! Still, with that knowing, planning can happen, and it's not a problem. Hell, why not plan! Once the "why" falls away, everything is done out of the "well, why not!?" It's very freeing.

Q. There doesn't seem to be the energy there to push something through. I can't do what I used to do in a sense. It's difficult being around ordinary everyday life, being around an ordinary family, and being that way.

Yes, it can be difficult for a while. But there's still a sense of separation there. That you are somehow different from them, somehow apart from "ordinary everyday life". That you're "being this way", and they aren't.

Q. They're not ordinary. It's just that life seems to be going on, the way it always did.

Yes, everything has changed, and yet nothing has changed. On the surface, a very ordinary life carries on. It's astonishing how ordinary it is. All of those ideas we had about awakening and enlightenment, they are seen to be just ideas. Actually, awakening is painfully ordinary! But right at the heart of that ordinariness, is this astonishing openness that allows that ordinary life to play itself out.

And of course, the secret is that it's not an ordinary life at all. It's quite extraordinary, but that can only be seen once the search for the extraordinary falls away. That whole ordinary/extraordinary paradox is resolved in the clarity of this seeing.

And there are no mistakes in Oneness. If a plan hasn't been made, then it shouldn't have been made. This is an absolute alignment with what is. It's a constant wonder. If a plan hasn't been made, then that's it! The plan shouldn't have been made! To the mind, this is almost madness. It's so simple. So simple. Too simple for the mind.

Q. A feeling comes back in, like I should be doing something. But if it's not happening, it's not happening.

That's it. That's it! The mind always wants something to *do*. It doesn't know any better. It keeps on wanting to improve your life, as if it was yours to improve! But what is given is already enough. It's already complete in that. There is no lack. There cannot possibly be any lack. The lack comes from the separate person who wants something. The wanting is the lacking. You know, the word "want" actually originates from the Old Norse word "vanta" which means "to lack"! So no wonder life never seems complete for the separate person who always wants something. Their wanting is creating the sense of lack!

In this, what is presented is all there is. And there are no mistakes. And it's astonishing, it's nothing like the mind thought it would be. So, a plan hasn't been made? It shouldn't have been made. The absolute simplicity of what is. And in the next moment, a plan may get made! There's no way of knowing. But right now, it hasn't been made. This is living in the not knowing. And everything comes out of that, it's the source of everything, including all plans. In that not knowing, things get done. Or not. But it cannot be understood. It's too simple to be understood.

People think that this is too complicated to be understood! But no, it's too *simple* to be understood.

Q. I feel that you must have some knowing that I don't have. You seem so steady and sure.

Oh no. If anything, I have less knowing! The drive to know this, to understand this, has fallen away.

Q. There's no need to know it anymore.

And that's the trust you talked about.

Q. It's the innocence.

Yes. And it was always innocent. Throughout the whole search. It all unfolded in absolute innocence.

And that's the true meaning of forgiveness. Nobody ever did anything to you. Nobody is to blame. It was all your dream, all your story. Everything happened in innocence, without any choice. And in that, the past is swept away, and you're left here, right here. This is where it all ends, and begins. It's a new beginning.

Life doesn't cease. We have this idea, that when this awakening happens, life somehow ceases. That it's some sort of full stop. But actually, it's a new beginning. Life is freed to live itself, in its fullness. There's nobody there who's fighting it anymore. So it can appear exactly as it is. And it appears as this now.

Q. So does nothing trouble you, once you are in that knowing?

Situations happen, and there's a response to them. But the heaviness goes out of it all.

Q. Feelings are still as strong, but you don't hold them?

When there's nobody there separate from life, sadness is allowed to be fully sad. Anger can be fully angry. But they just burn themselves up. Because there's nobody there anymore trying to *do* anything with anger, trying to *do* anything with sadness. There's nobody there trying to get an identity out of being an angry *person*, being a sad *person*, or even being a spiritual *person*. That's the beauty of this, it's an openness in which anything can happen. It allows anything to arise and dissolve. And there's a beautiful lightness to it. The heaviness goes. The heaviness was always the separate person, wanting something from life.

Q. And the guilt, and trying to be good?

It all goes. It ceases to mean anything anymore. The seeing that this is all there is, is the same as seeing that everything, the whole past, unravelled in absolute innocence. That it couldn't have been any other way. It couldn't have been any other way. Because nobody was doing it. There was no choice. That destroys all guilt.

Q. Is that an intellectual knowing? I mean, if *this* is so, then *that* had to be so?

It could appear that way. Actually, it's nothing to do with the intellect. This is happening. And the past arises in this, as a story. And it couldn't be otherwise. The past is the story of the past.

Q. Of course. The past is a story.

Yes. It's amazing how solid it can seem. And in a moment, it's gone. When the thought isn't there, the past isn't there. And it's still allowed to arise, as a story.

And then you can tell the *story* of the past. That's all we ever do really, tell the story of the past. And that releases it. It releases the whole thing.

Q. Sometimes it's like being in a movie. I was sitting having a conversation the other day, and felt like bursting into laughter. There were people talking to each other, but it was all seen to be a movie. It's amazing.

And the beauty of it is that it's not a movie that you're watching. You're not separate from the movie. You're fully involved in it, and yet you're not there. It's completely impersonal, and yet it's wonderfully personal, and intimate. There's a real intimacy to it. And in the movie, anything can happen. Sad scenes, happy scenes. And yet it's just a movie, and when that's seen, the heaviness goes out of it.

And that's what it always was: a movie. And the movie exists to be seen. To be seen. You don't sit in a cinema, trying to do something with the movie! No, it's there to be seen. And in the simplicity of that seeing, everything is released to be exactly what it is.

Q. When you walk out of the cinema you don't take the movie with you.

Exactly. And yet, part of the enjoyment of going to see a movie, is in pretending that it's real.

It *seems* so wonderfully real. The living is in the *seeming*.

~

Q. What do you feel is the importance of spiritual practices? I appreciate that the idea of a path is me trying to reach somewhere. But I also feel that there is a place for certain practices, for some people. Practices do seem to have an effect. For example, if I'd had several pints of beer before coming here, I wouldn't be listening to what you were saying.

Oh, I had several pints of beer before coming here!
(Laughter)

Q. But in terms of actually being able to listen to the words that you're saying, do spiritual practices have their place in terms of helping the mind? You mentioned that this message can be challenging for some people. Wouldn't spiritual practices help to open them up, so to speak, and enable them to hear this message more clearly?

Everything has its place in this. If you find yourself doing spiritual practices, that's exactly what's supposed to be happening. But over here, when this was seen, the spiritual practices fell away of their own accord. Because it was seen that the person doing the meditation, doing the self-enquiry, simply wasn't there. And in the seeing that nobody does these practices, they can fall away of their own accord.

Or not. But there's no way of knowing right now.

That *isn't* the same as saying "give up your spiritual practices". That's how this message may be heard though. But that would miss the point entirely, you see. The point is, the practising goes on, until it doesn't anymore. You know, I practised until I was blue in the face. I did everything. But as long as there was practising, there was a separate "me" with goals. I meditated in order to reach a peaceful state. I self-enquired in order to get to the root of the "I" thought. As long as I believed I was a separate person, I never felt complete, and so there was practising in order to escape the prison of individuality. It was a vicious circle. And at the time, *that's what I needed*! There are no mistakes!

Q. Some people who appear to be enlightened still carry on with their spiritual practices. I suppose there's the sense of *why not*, I mean if there's nothing better to do!

You cannot know what will happen when this is seen. Spiritual practices could continue. You might become the greatest meditator in the world! Or you could find yourself never touching another spiritual teaching ever again. That's what happened over here. I never touched anything to do with spirituality ever again. It all became meaningless to me. Ordinary life was always more than enough, and the idea of the "spiritual" as opposed to the "material" was seen to be a false duality.

But that's not a prescription. That was just what unfolded over here. And nor is this about condemning spiritual practices. Everything has its place in this. This isn't about giving up. The point is, you don't have a choice.

195

Q. It's incredibly strange. When you were speaking just then, there was a sense that everything here and now is complete. And I felt very, very close. But not quite there. There was a little bit of reaching out still happening, which somehow added to this sense of completeness and obviousness. The added bit seems to be the challenge. And yet I know it's not a challenge...

There seems to be a momentum to the seeking. The mind cannot stay with this clarity for long. And so the "added bit" surges back in, and tries to keep the seeking going. To the mind, this is a life-or-death struggle. The poor little mind always wants something to do. It loves its paths and processes. It loves its intellectual understanding. It wants an identity. It wants to be a person who gets this!

Actually, all there is, is this. And in this, the mind does what it does. There's a little bit of grasping going on. And you're not doing that. If you were doing that, you would choose to stop the grasping right now. The point is, you are not doing it. It's all unfolding in Oneness. This is freedom from the burden of volition.

Q. So you don't have any choice?

No, no choice. There's no choice in this. Did you choose to nod your head just then?

Q. No. *(Laughter)*

It's that simple. It's so simple. It's always overlooked by a seeking mind. To the mind, the miracle can't be *here*. It has to be *out there*. And yet, this miracle allows the mind to carry on seeking. It allows the grasping to play itself out. It allows the mind to come back in, and fight for superiority. The mind always goes "I'm not there yet!" That is its mantra. But even that is just a thought. That's all it could possibly be.

And the mind gets more and more subtle. It's always whispering in the background "you're not there yet, you're not there yet!" And that's always happening where you are. You're here, and the mind's going "you're not there yet, you're not there yet!"
(Laughter)

And that's its function. That's its job. It doesn't know what else to do. Really, the mind has no clue.

Q. So the trick is to hear what you're saying, but not do anything with it.

Or if you find yourself doing something about it, that's okay too.

Q. Yes, because that's what's happening.

Yes. It's not really about the words. It's not about the understanding of this. But I guess that if you're here, and you haven't run out of the room screaming yet, there's already a resonance happening, and it's nothing to do with the words. Really, what's happening here is Oneness meeting Oneness and delighting in that. And in that meeting, all the questions of the mind begin to dissolve, because it's seen in clarity that everything's already complete. And then what's left to do but play with stories?

Q. The mind does get very worried about having nothing to do.

It does. In its innocence. You see, to the mind, having nothing to do is death! "In the absence of something to do, who am I?" To the mind, that's death. Death of the individual. But actually, death is liberation.

All that happens on physical death, is the falling away of the doing, the falling away of the story of "me". The falling away of the struggle. So of course, the mind cannot hear this message! It doesn't want to hear about its own death! *(Laughter)*

This is why I say that *you* would never have chosen to come here. The mind would never have chosen to come to this meeting today, and hear about its own death! So this has nothing to do with you. You haven't brought yourself here today. You wouldn't want to come and hear this. I wouldn't want to come and talk about this. Oneness is doing this, not us.

And so it becomes obvious that we're constantly being cradled by Oneness. It mothers us. It does everything for us. There's nothing we have to do. That's the real meaning of "doing nothing". It's not about giving up what you're already doing. It's not about giving up beliefs or religions. The point is, there's nothing you need to do, because it's already being done. *The Lord is my shepherd, I shall not want.* God is always taking care of you, if you want to use religious words.

And oh, the absolute simplicity of that! Right now, it's providing us with chairs to sit on. And air to breathe. And a floor to hold us up. And clothes to keep us warm. And to the mind, that's way too simple, far too simplistic. Because the mind goes "I did this! I bought the clothes! I chose to come here and sit down!" And so we move so far away from that simple, natural gratitude at what is. Without the story of choice, without the story that you did any of this, it's like... wow! It's *being done*! Wow, there's a chair there, holding me up. And there's a cushion on it so I'm comfortable. And there's clothes keeping me warm. And hair growing on my arm. And fingernails to protect the tips of my fingers. This is grace, and it is beyond religion, beyond spirituality. It's beyond all concepts of awakening, liberation and enlightenment. This is such a rare message. And yet, it's not really rare at all. It's everywhere.

Without the story of a past, it's like... oh, look! I've got shoes on my feet! Look, there's hair on my head! And money in my pocket! And without the story of a past, without the story of how you got here... look what's *given*! Look what it's *giving*! Look what's *there*! Without any effort. It's given freely.

Sounds to listen to. Sights to see. Smells to smell. It doesn't have to give this, but it does. It's giving you sensations in the body. It doesn't have to! It's giving you air to breathe. It doesn't have to! It gives all of this freely, asking nothing of you. And it gives it constantly. It's unconditional love, all of it.

And it doesn't stop there. On top of all this, it gives you a story. The story of an outside world! It gives you places to go. You can walk outside, and go shopping, and sit on park benches and watch the world go by. And you can go home to your families, and chat on the phone to your friends, and weep at old movies, and so on and so on. It's almost too much! Not only does it give you *this*, which is enough, but it gives you all of *that* too! An apparent outside world to play with!

In our innocence we've been looking for so much more. And it was always *given*. And it cannot be lost. There's not even the possibility of that. Because it's not yours. Because it cannot be possessed, because it belongs to nobody, because it's given freely, it cannot be lost.

And a moment before death this will be the case. You'll be lying there on your hospital bed, and there will be nurses looking after you, and a soft bed to sleep on, and a pillow to rest your head on, and medicine to take away the pain, and people who love you will be in tears. See, it's given. It's already given. That's why it's called unconditional love. It's unconditional, asking nothing of you. That's how much it loves you.

And if this abundance isn't seen yet, it's even giving you the *possibility* of seeing it! That's how much it loves you. Because you're not separate from it, and that's what the word "love" points to. The end of separation. The end of war.

~

Q. You said that if you had no memory of the past, then you're right here, and you've got money in your pocket

but you've no idea where it came from. I don't understand it, but it resonates. It feels very profound.

Without the story of what this is, without knowing what this is, without the past, what *is* this? We've never actually seen it. We're too busy knowing it. "Oh, I'm just a person, sitting on a chair. So what!" That's the story of the past. That's the "me".

Without that story, there's no way of knowing what this is. So this is a constant discovery. You see it for the first time. "Oh, look, I've got two of these funny things with strange little appendages, and oh, they're called *hands*! Wow, I've got hands so I can hold things, and feet so I can walk, and ears so I can hear!" It's like being born again. Seeing the world for the first time. And in that, there's a natural gratitude, and the seeking ends. And the whole spiritual search is based on the assumption that this – what's already *given* – isn't enough.

Q. That this moment isn't enough.

Yes. Why else would we search?

Q. Yes, that's what we do all the time. That's why we put money away for the future. We are frightened of what will happen otherwise.

Yes, and it's no wonder that this search only ever ends in frustration. Because actually the search is fuelled by lack. So anywhere the seeking takes you, underneath it all is the sense of separation, the sense of lack, the sense that this isn't enough. We project lack *everywhere*.

There is essentially no difference between getting something, and forgetting that you want something. In both the *getting* and the for-*getting* there is absence of seeking, which, paradoxically, is what we really want. The getting and forgetting are just reflections of each other.

But we believe that it's *because* we got the new car that we're feeling contentment. Actually, for a moment, the seeking for the car dropped, and really that's got nothing to do with the car! When you get the car, the attempt to get the car drops momentarily, and that's the contentment you experience. But the same contentment would also arise from forgetting that you wanted the car in the first place! It's the same movement of mind. So you can bypass the car, and save yourself some money, and come to rest now!

In other words, you don't need to get what you want to be free. The freedom is in the falling away of seeking. And that is possible here and now, not in a future time. And in the seeing of that, *this* is always what you want. And it's always given. It's the only want that could ever be satisfied permanently! It's an absolute alignment with what is.

And yet the seeking happens in total innocence. There's no condemnation of seeking here. We just didn't know any better at the time.

Q. The seeking appears to stop you appreciating what's here now.

And yet really the seeking stops nothing. The search isn't a block. The mind thinks that the seeking is a block to seeing this. That's the tactic it uses to keep itself going. It starts to seek for the end of seeking!

You see, seeking is allowed in this. It's allowed to happen. The point is that you're not doing it. It's not a problem. And when that's seen, the seeking burns itself up, funnily enough. This *seeing* destroys all *seeking*.

And actually, this is already seen. No need for a future. It's being seen now. It's all there is. It's all that's happening. And actually everything happens *within* this seeing. So the seeing is always there. It's been there from the beginning. That's all that's happening here today.

Words are happening, sounds are happening, but really all of this is just a play happening *within* the clarity. So really the seeking doesn't obscure the clarity. It can't. It's *part* of the clarity.

The seeking isn't the enemy. There's no enemy. It's all One.

Part Two

Q. Sometimes we say that this manifestation is "apparent". Is it because it constantly *appears* here?

Yes, that's what the word "apparent" is pointing to. The manifestation is what *appears*. And the question is, to whom does it appear? Well, it appears for nobody. But that isn't an intellectual understanding. It's a clear seeing.

And language breaks down right there, you see. That's the problem with talking about nonduality! Once you talk about an appearance, you're talking about *something* appearing to *someone*, to an entity. And actually, there is no entity. And so really there is no appearance!

So you can only really talk *around* this. You can't capture it in words. The words are just pointers, and what the words are pointing to is a plunge into something that's totally beyond words.

Q. So does an appearance always have to arise for *someone*? When you talk to us, do you see an "us"?

The moment you talk about it, it appears as though there's someone talking to someone else. Beyond all words, beyond thought, beyond understanding, this is happening. And the mind comes in and goes "I see this". So the moment we talk about it we're into our stories. The point is, it's just happening. It's too simple to talk about. That's why I say that a newborn baby sees this. A newborn baby isn't yet lost in these stories. It's not trying to work out to whom the

appearance appears!
(Laughter)

Or maybe it is!
(Laughter)

Q. When we say "apparent" it sounds like something's not real. But at the same time, it all seems so real, so solid.

Oh, it's supposed to seem solid. That's the play. It's supposed to be convincing.

Q. It's amazing though, having something so real, and knowing that it's not real, but having to live *as if* it is real. It's like a cosmic joke. It's almost schizophrenic!
(Laughter)

Q. It's like walking on a tightrope. You have to involve yourself. You can't sit back. But then again, you can't really do anything!

Yes, it cannot be understood. And all of these questions just fall away. "How do I deal with it? How do I get involved? Should I try to remain detached? What will become of me?" They just fall away. It just does itself.

And really, you only ever have to deal with this, with what's happening, with the present moment. And this is always okay. The Zen master Rinzai used to ask "In this moment, what is lacking?"

Q. And whether or not this is real or unreal... that's just

more thoughts coming in, isn't it?

Yes, it's a game! And it gets very serious sometimes. All those intellectual arguments! Is it real, is it unreal, and so on. And the beauty of this, is that it doesn't have to be understood. It's not about understanding whether it's real or not. And yet, that game can go on. But it can be seen: it's not serious! It's just a game!

Ultimately, it's not real or unreal. It is what it is. And it can't be known. And it doesn't need to be known. It's just presenting itself. And it doesn't ask to be known! This chair, it's just presenting itself. It's not asking to be known. It's just... here. Present. Simple. Showing itself.

You know, that's the real meaning of the word "enlightenment". To bring into the light. To be shown. To be lit up. And you know, it's already being shown. It's already in the light, it's already showing itself, it's already being revealed. Right now, this is Oneness revealing itself. It's always revealing itself. A constant revelation.

So this is enlightenment. The chair is already seen in enlightenment. It doesn't need to be understood. Those intellectual games we play are just distractions. But the attempt to understand goes hand in hand with the lack of understanding we apparently experience. And the mind thinks that to get rid of the lack of understanding, it needs to try and understand. And that's exactly how it keeps the lack of understanding going, and in that, keeps itself alive. The lack of understanding *is* the attempt to understand. It's the same movement.

And every newborn baby sees this. And they see it because they aren't trying to see it! And that's all we are. We're newborn babies. Newborn babies with this thing called a past, which, on closer, inspection, is just a story.

Q. And we're not even that. That's just something you're saying right now.

Yes. The moment you talk about it, you've made it into something.

Q. Everything's happening here.

Yes, and that includes anything. Everything. Anything can happen here. This is total openness to what is. Everything is allowed to happen. Nothing is stopping this from happening! So there's nothing you have to do to make this happen. It's completely free. That's why it's called freedom. If it wasn't free, it wouldn't be called *freedom*.

Q. And we say it's One, because it always happens here.

Yes. We're not separate from it. It's always here. It's One. And it's already complete. It doesn't need anything else. And it's nothing like we ever thought it would be! Awakening, or this, or whatever you want to call it, it's nothing like you thought it would be.

You know, I had so many ideas about awakening and enlightenment. I was stuffed full of them. So many ideas, so many concepts, from all the books I'd read, from all the teachings. It was shocking to see that it was just this. To a mind so full of baggage, the simplicity of this was shocking. Because, in this simplicity, what use do all the teachings of the world have? All the teachings of the world burn up in this.

Q. You mentioned freedom. The idea of "me" disappearing can be quite terrifying. But at the same time, there's the sense that if the "me" disappears, then there's nobody controlling what's going on… and that can be terrifying too!

Oh yes, it's the "me" trying to work it all out. I was terrified of this too, for ages! But what was there to fear? There's just this. Nothing to fear here.

Q. Well, you appear to be quite sensible…

That's what you think!
(Laughter)

Q. But there's this idea that if the "me" disappears, then you could do all sorts of crazy things.

And again, that's the mind trying to hold on. "When there's no "me", I could do anything, I might go crazy! Or perhaps I'll just crumple in a heap on the floor and do nothing!" The fear is the mind trying to protect itself.

Q. I suppose the question is, when the "me" goes, what looks after things?

What looks after things, is that which is asking that question. That which is allowing all of this to happen now. It's all already being looked after.

There is nothing to fear. There is only the fear. Present fear arising, but nothing to be afraid *of.* That's the mind's mantra: "something to fear, something to fear!" It's the mind getting desperate. It tries to use the intellect to grasp this, and when that fails, it tries the fear tactic.

Q. But life seems so well-ordered. What you're suggesting is that Oneness is actually looking after it all.

Yes. It's astonishing really. There's nobody here doing this, and yet this body wakes in the morning, brushes its teeth, has breakfast, and so on. And it's the constant mystery. Nobody's doing it, but everything gets done. You know, the mind says "without me, you're nothing!" But what does the mind know? In that nothing, there's *everything.*

It's what beats the heart. It's what moves the planets. It's what keeps birds in formation. It's what breaks your heart, and moves you to tears. It's the unknowable mystery of the universe. And it's not separate from anything else.

This is a life lived in fullness. Because there's nobody there anymore who's separate from life, nobody trying to *do* anything with it. The emptiness is filled with sounds and sounds and feelings. And there's a great intimacy to it. You know, there's this idea that once you awaken – and *you* cannot awaken – nothing will touch you. Your mother could die, and it wouldn't touch you. What utter bullshit. When this is seen, everything is released, so everything can be itself. Sadness can be fully sad. You could cry for days at the death of a loved one. Because you're no longer separate from what happens, there are no rules. It's a life lived in absolute openness, which is absolute rawness. And the sadness can tear you apart. But right at the heart of that sadness, everything is okay. Right at the heart of that sadness, there can be great laughter.

You're supposed to be sad when someone dies, right? Well yes, there can be great sadness. But there can be great laughter too. To the mind, this sounds like madness. Actually it's absolute freedom. Total intimacy. Your friend dying or your mother dying is yourself. There is no separation. And so there is an equanimity that permeates everything. And that equanimity allows the sadness to be fully sad. You could weep oceans of tears. And then the sadness dissolves, and the freshness is there again. It's like the sadness never happened. Everything is wiped clean, because there is no solid "me" that endures from one experience to the next. So there's nobody there clinging onto the identity of a "sad person". There is just sadness passing through, but no sad person there.

So, life doesn't become "perfect". It becomes very raw. It's a life stripped of mythology.

Q. Did you have a dramatic disappearing of "Jeff"?

It's hard to talk about. My spiritual search reached a point of such intensity that it became incredibly unpleasant and serious. But then, in the midst of that seriousness there was a clear seeing that I simply wasn't there.

I desperately wanted to become enlightened. And I had such a ferocious intellect. I read everything, devoured book after book. I never went to any spiritual meetings though. This all took place at home. I sat in the garden of my parents' house for about a year, mainly just staring at things! My cat Tangy used to accompany me. You know, back then I really didn't know what was going on. But I never spoke to anyone about what I was going through. My family didn't even know what the word "spirituality" meant! So I was very alone at that time.

All I can say is that the seeking exhausted itself, and fell away.

Q. Was there a definite knowing that "Jeff" wasn't there anymore?

There were times when it was seen with absolute clarity that I wasn't there. And sometimes this seeing would last a few minutes, sometimes for a few hours, sometimes for days. And then the mind would come back in, and the seeking would go on. "I experienced something, now how do I get it back?" And so the misery continued. Waiting for this ultimate point of awakening, where I would permanently disappear. It became so serious. I shut myself away from the world.

For a while, and I can't say for how long it lasted, the "I" came and went and came back again. And the seeking became more and more subtle, until eventually, it no longer mattered whether "Jeff" was there or not. And then it was all over. It was a total giving up of the search. It's not that I found what I was looking for. The search just gave itself up, eventually. It was nothing that I could have brought about through effort.

It's not dependent on how old you are, on your education, on your background. Some people say that you have to seek for thirty, forty years to get this. That's absolutely ridiculous. Freedom has no requirements.

This had nothing to do with anything that I'd done. That was seen clearly. It had nothing to do with my ferocious intellect. If anything, that had only intensified the seeking.

You know, my cat saw this! For all that time I spent in the garden, my cat would just sit there next to me. And it would be a beautiful sunny day, and I would be lost in my concepts of enlightenment, staring at a flower and waiting for enlightenment to descend, and my cat would just sit there, looking up at me, wondering what the hell I was doing!
(Laughter)

So really, my cat was my teacher.
(Laughter)

Unfortunately, she's dead now, so you can't meet her!
(Laughter)

Q. So these days, there can be periods when "Jeff" is there?

Even if there were, it wouldn't matter. There is no seeking here anymore. No desire for anything other than what's happening. And even the idea that "Jeff" can be there or not, really it makes no sense to me, I just use those words in response to your question. There is just what is, and nothing more. If "Jeff" happens to be there, he is a welcome friend. And when I say "Jeff", I just mean thought. That's all there is. Presently arising thought. And when thought is not there, Jeff is not there. Simple.

You see, this happened in spite of the mind's failure to get what it wanted. In a sense, awakening is spiritual failure. The failure of the mind.

And then the seriousness goes out of it. It can get so serious. You know, it got to the point where I couldn't even have a normal conversation with someone. Years ago I went for a walk in the park with my mum, who's a very exuberant American. She loves nature, and she pointed at a tree and said "Isn't that tree beautiful, Jeff?" And I looked at her, angry as hell, and said "Mum, there's no such thing as a tree!"
(Laughter)

I said it in all seriousness. I was angry at her for being lost in the dream world. For being completely un-enlightened!
(Laughter)

I said "Mum, there's no such thing as beauty! That's just a label! That's just the mind!"
(Laughter)

That's how serious this spiritual seeking can get. What I couldn't see then, was that the ego was stronger than *ever*! I thought that I was free from ego. So be wary of anyone who tells you they're free from ego! They probably feel superior to you, and that's more ego than ever.

(Laughter)

Of course, there was a truth to what I said. But it came from a place where this truth had not yet been integrated, and there was still a feeling of being separate from others.

Q. So how did your mother take this?

Oh, poor woman. She took it all very well though. I think she sensed that something was happening to me, something I couldn't explain.

When this is seen, there is so much laughter. The seriousness goes out of everything, and there is just laughter. It's such a relief. But everything is still honoured. It doesn't mean that you go round laughing *at* everything!
(Laughter)

Actually, when the seriousness goes out of everything, you still find yourself doing what needs to be done. It doesn't mean that you sit back and do nothing. If there's an emergency, for example, or what the world calls an emergency anyway, you do what needs to be done. Without the stress, without the pity, without the fear.

Here's another example of how serious the seeking can get. Years ago, my brother told me off for not doing the washing up. I told him, again in all seriousness, that the "me" who didn't do the washing up didn't even exist, that he was talking about a "me" of the past, and so he was confused!
(Laughter)

So you see, I've done this seeking thing!

Q. So nobody could ever argue back?

Yes, I always won my arguments! But really I was always left feeling very isolated.

Then again, I had no choice in all of this. The seeking had to run its course. Once the fire in me began, I had no choice. It had to burn itself out.

Q. You said that at one point you didn't care whether "Jeff" was there or not. So it didn't matter whether pain was there, or happiness was there, or whatever.

Yes. The futility of wanting anything other than what was happening, was seen. And when that's seen, the energy goes out of the seeking, out of the caring. That energy is released. Undoubtedly the seeking drains so much energy!

Q. So whatever is there isn't a problem. You're not attached to what arises. If there's happiness, it comes and goes, and you're not attached to it.

Yes. There can be a lot of laughter when that's seen.

Q. There's no interest in whether your body appears or not?

No interest. It's there when it's there, and when it's not, it's not. It's that simple. It's too simple to hear!

Q. So is the body there now?

This (slaps leg) is here. You know, I spent years trying to understand this intellectually. Am I the body? In what does the body arise? Why does Oneness manifest as this body and not that one? The questions went on and on, and I got so lost in this attempt to understand what is so utterly simple. I missed the simplicity of *this (slaps leg)*! In the simplicity of this, all questions dissolve.

Awakening isn't a state that you enter. It's a clear seeing of what's already there. Of what was there throughout all the seeking. And in that seeing, you are destroyed. And in the absence of you, there is a fullness, an aliveness, but it's not a cold, grey, dead absence. It's a very alive absence, filled with sights and sounds and smells, and floors, and ceilings, and windows...

Q. And the body, right?

Yes.

Q. And it has the same importance as the floor or the window.

Yes. Equal. This is absolute equality. In Zen they call it *One Taste*.

Q. Sometimes when I'm with people, I can't distinguish which body is mine.

Years ago, when I lived in Oxford, I got on a bus once, and the bus conductor asked me for some money, and I had no idea who he was talking to! I couldn't work out if he was talking to me, or if I was talking to him, or if I was talking to myself. It can be very odd when this is first seen.

Because there's nothing here, whatever is presented in the moment, that's what I am. The absence over here is filled up with sights and sounds and smells, and faces and bodies and all sorts. The mind gets hooked on this idea that when the separate self falls away, there will be nothing. But that's because the mind thinks it's everything, and when everything goes, there will be nothing! "In the absence of me, there will be nothing!" Actually, in the absence of me, there's everything, in its fullness.

Q. You just said that when there's pain, it's felt here. But pain is not felt in this body, it's just felt.

Yes. But there is still simple physical location. Pain appears in *this* foot rather than in *that* foot. It's that simple.

Q. But sometimes you can feel the pain of someone else. When they are suffering, sometimes you can feel it.

When the idea of separation goes, it's not surprising that you can feel the pain of "others"! I was on the train with my girlfriend a few weeks ago. I went to go to the bathroom, and there was a guy standing there waiting, and I politely asked him if he was waiting for the bathroom. For no reason, he began shouting violently at me. There was real anger there. But it wasn't his. And it wasn't mine. Anger was happening for no one. And I could tell the story that I felt his anger. But really there was only the anger, and it was nobody's. It was like the Universe was anger-ing. It was just a play of energy.

And really the seeing of that, is what we might call "compassion". The word "compassion" literally means "to suffer along with". To see that my suffering is not separate from your suffering. So, in compassion, you meet that angry man, and see that it's not my anger or his anger. It's anger happening. It's Oneness in the form of an angry man. It's just energy. It's not essentially real. It's just a cartoon man on a cartoon train, displaying cartoon anger.

It's a profound insight: that we don't "feel" the pain of others, because there are no others. There is just the feeling of the pain, by no one. Well of course there is, because we're not separate! The pain is experienced in emptiness, and we tell the story "it's his pain as opposed to my pain". But the pain does not belong to anyone, and the seeing of that releases the whole damn thing. The non-attachment to anger forces the anger to burn itself out. It has nothing to cling to anymore, nowhere to rest.

Years ago, this guy's anger would have made me angry, and I would have blamed him for making me angry, and blamed the world for being unenlightened and prone to anger. I would have taken the anger away with me. Done something with it, probably. In the seeing that anger happens for no one, all of that violence falls away.

Q. Sometimes you suddenly feel that somebody is with you, when they're not physically present.

Yes, there are no separate people. There's only the *story* of mother, father, sister, brother, friend and so on. And those stories arise here. They are always *here*.

Q. It's as if you know that they're present.

You only have your stories. So, say your friend Gary walks into the room. All you have is your story of Gary. You see the physical form, and you tell the story of Gary. And even if Gary is on the other side of the world, that's all you have. Your story of Gary, and the feelings that go along with that. So you see, Gary is always *here*, he's never *there*. He's always with you, in this intimacy. We just tell the story that he's on the other side of the world, to keep the separation game going. He is what you are. You are not separate.

Q. That's where I get completely lost. Sometimes, even though you don't know they're around, you have a sense of someone, and then they appear.

Where do they appear?

Q. Physically. Sometimes they physically appear.

So let's make someone appear now, then!
(Laughter)

Q. It happens especially after these meetings, when I'm especially in tune. Somehow you know someone's about to walk into the room, and then they do, and you had no way of knowing that they would.

It's all energy. Strange things happen when that is seen.

There are no separate people. So really, knowing that someone's about to walk into the room, and that person then walking into the room, is part of the same movement of energy. When the separate person falls away, there is an astonishing sensitivity to what is. But it would be a mistake to make any of these experiences "special", and call them "psychic abilities" and so on. These experiences are unsurprising when the sense of being separate falls away.

Even to say that you sense that a separate person is going to come into the room, that's still part of the dream. There is no person coming into the room. It's a movement of thought. Really, your *story* is coming into the room. Which means, they're already *here*. Everyone you know is already here. They're right here in this room. They haven't paid to get in though, the buggers! *(Laughter)*

Look, say your father walks into the room. Really, you have no idea what's just walked into the room. You see that physical form and you say "father" and tell that story. That's the story that's arisen every time that being has walked into the room. Actually, there is no father. Or, as Jesus said, I and the Father are One.

Q. I see that the whole world is going on in my head. It's all me, it's all coming from the same source.

In the East, many religions talk about the fact that you are God. Brahman is Atman, and so on. The Universe arises in you. And it arises as a thought. And when the thought isn't there, the Universe isn't there. See, you create and destroy a whole Universe in a thought! That's how amazing you are! *(Laughter)*

No, this can get muddled up with all that New Age stuff about manifesting your destiny, and the ego can swell to gargantuan proportions when it hears that it's God. No, that would be to miss the point of this entirely. The point is, "you" cannot create anything, but also you are not separate from creation!

Because we have our story of mother, father, sister, brother, we don't *see*. To *see* that being in front of you without your story, that's to meet in Oneness. In that, there is no separation. And in that, they are always with you. They can never leave you. They cannot die. And anyone who's ever loved anyone, and lost them, has a sense of that. When you love someone absolutely, they cannot die. The physical body falls away of course, but they cannot die. Even people who have no interest in spirituality have that sense. *Love is as strong as death.*

⁓

Q. Do you see everything as happening in the present? Sometimes the mind believes things that aren't happening in the present.

Really there's no such thing as the present. To know *this* as the present, you have to know *that* as the past or future. But the past and future are always just thoughts happening now.

Actually, to say that everything happens in the present, means that there is no present at all. To the mind, everything exists in opposition, and so if everything is present, then there is no present, because there is nothing that opposes the present. This is the world of apparent duality.

In other words, the present needs the past and future to be known as the present. If everything is present, then there is no past and future, and so there is no present.

Q. Okay, but when you're absorbed in thoughts about the past or future, it can be quite unpleasant.

Even absorption in the past and future is okay. It's allowed in this. The unpleasantness is actually just something else happening. There's sights and sounds and smells, and people walking down the street, and the heart beating, and breathing, and unpleasantness happening. And unpleasantness comes and goes.

The problem comes when the mind goes "damn, I'm feeling unpleasant, I've lost presence!" As if presence was something that came and went. But even in the midst of the most unpleasant unpleasantness, it can be seen that it's all just a present appearance. And that releases it.

Presence isn't a state. That's a misunderstanding of what the word points to. When we say "I was present" what we really mean is *"I wasn't there." When you're truly present, you're not there.*

Q. And you can't put yourself there. But it can just happen.

Yes. And actually we're already there. It's all that's happening. It's happening now. It's that which is allowing this conversation to happen. It even allows the individual to go off and seek presence! Even the search for presence happens within presence. The beauty of presence is that it cannot be owned. You can't have it. It's not a state that you can access, it's what's already there, and that can be revealed when the seeking for it dies away.

Stories are allowed to arise in presence. For years I wanted to get rid of my stories. A story was trying to end a story! But really stories are not the enemy. They are allowed to arise in this. Everything is allowed to arise in this. Stories are as present as anything else.

So, if you're not feeling present, that's exactly what's supposed to be happening. In presence, an individual believes they are not present. And that belief comes and goes. So when that seeking for presence dies away, it reveals itself. When it's ready. Not when you're ready. It's very strange and wonderful.

Q. There's nothing to do, and nowhere to go. And yes, that appears to be true. It's really the opposite of what we'd expect, isn't it!

Oh yes, it's the last thing we'd ever expect! And yet, when this message is heard, you don't understand it intellectually but there's a resonance there, and it's Oneness resonating with itself. It's nothing to do with the mind. It cannot be understood, it cannot be taught. But somehow, it can be shared. And that's all that's happening here. A sharing of what's already known.

There's nothing new here. We've always known this. From the very beginning we've known this. As newborn babies we knew this. Since before the Big Bang we've known this.

DIALOGUE FIVE

An Ordinary Awakening

Earth, mountains, rivers,
hidden in this nothingness.

In this nothingness,
earth, mountains, rivers revealed.

Spring flowers, winter snows.
There's no being or non-being,
nor denial itself.

Saisho

Part One

This is about the possibility that the seeking game, the game the mind plays to keep itself alive, can fall away. And of course the moment we say that, the mind latches onto it. "I want that! I want the end of seeking!" And the end of seeking has become the new goal. The mind loves its goals.

It's the last thing the mind wants to hear: this is already Oneness. And there's nothing you have to do to reach Oneness. It's already happening. The heart's beating. Sounds are happening. Breathing is happening. And you're not doing it. That's the illusion, that you're in control. The mind comes in and goes "I'm doing it! I'm hearing! I'm seeing! I'm thinking!" So the mind's always grasping. It wants to be in charge. And it can get very threatened by a message which exposes its little games.

But this is so far beyond anything the mind could ever grasp. What we are trying to point to is a spontaneous play of energy, of Oneness, of God, of Spirit. All those words are pointing to the same thing. The same no-thing!

Life is just happening. It's always just happening. And it doesn't need you. It's already complete, in itself. It asks nothing of you. And when all that effort to become something, to improve myself, to change myself, when all of that falls away it's seen so clearly that it's already complete, as it is. And in that, there can still be a person there who lives their life. But the seriousness goes out of it. The heaviness goes out of it. It doesn't mean that you sit back and do nothing. It means that life lives itself.

But this isn't a new belief system to be taken on. All of this can be *seen* with absolute clarity. And then the questions fall away, and the confusion drops. And like newborn babies, we see the world for the first time. And in fact we're always seeing it for the first time, but that freshness can be somewhat clouded over by the seeking of the mind. The mind goes "This is nothing special. I've seen all of this before. It's so ordinary. It's just a room. Just a bunch of people listening to someone else talk." To the mind, it's all so ordinary, so known. But actually what's happening here, is Oneness playing. Seeing itself. Delighting in meeting itself in a thousand different forms. And this meeting is always happening. It's always meeting itself. Everything is a meeting in nonduality. But we can never see that, because we're looking for it!

You are just a thought. And that's the freedom, right there. The freedom isn't *out there*, somewhere in the future. It's always right at the heart of everything. It's constantly revealing itself. And when that's seen, all questions, all seeking dies away naturally. You cannot choose to stop seeking. It just falls away when it's ready. Not when you're ready! Because ultimately you're not doing this. Life is just living itself through you. Through what you call "you". It's what beats your heart. It's what breathes. Thoughts arise out of nowhere. Sounds come out of nowhere. The miracle is that out of nothing, everything is appearing. Right now. Wherever you are.

And it's all so ordinary. That's the funny thing about this. Liberation is so ordinary. It appears as a room full of people, now. That's how ordinary it is! But when the search for the extraordinary falls away, it's seen that this was always extraordinary. It was always right here, at the heart of things.

This isn't about the questions and the answers. And yet the questions and answers play themselves out. Until, finally, the questions stop. And then there's just... this. And nobody there to know it.

~

Q. Considering there's just this, what's doing the seeking?

Nothing's doing the seeking. There's no entity doing the seeking. That's the *illusion*.

Q. But it appears that way.

Yes, it appears that way. But when you really look, it's just not there. Everything just happens. And in the simplicity of that *happening*, the question is resolved. The mind cannot grasp that, because it can only think in terms of things, or entities. So when I say that everything's just happening, the mind goes "Yes, but who's doing it? Who's in charge?" That's just another tactic the mind uses, to keep itself going. Seeking the root of itself. The mind could never see that this is just a spontaneous play, and there's no entity at its centre. That's why I call it Life Without A Centre.

The mind cannot stay with the simplicity of what's happening for long. The questions soon begin: "Why is it happening? Who's doing it?" and so on. But it's just a spontaneous play. And a play doesn't need to be understood. Just *seen*.

Q. But it doesn't appear that way, does it? At the end of this meeting I'll get on my bike and ride home. That seems like a choice I'm going to make.

Yes, it seems like a choice! Actually, where we always are is the Unknown. There's no way of knowing where you'll be in a moment's time, in five seconds' time, in five days' time. There's no way of knowing what will happen. You can't know what will come out of the Unknown. And yet, the mind wants to know. Wants to think it makes choices.

You cannot really know that after the meeting you'll ride your bike home. But, if after the meeting, you find yourself riding your bike home, the mind will go "I'm doing this! I chose this! I knew this was going to happen!" So the story of choice is very convincing.

~

Q. You mentioned the story of choice being convincing. But who is it convincing to?

To the individual who thinks they are separate.

Q. Is there an individual?

Look, ask most people if they're an individual, and they will say yes. So we could say, there *appears* to be an individual. There's the story of choice. There's the story of past and future. There's no need to deny that those stories arise, that the individual arises in this. But what I'm saying, is that it's just a story arising now, arising in this. And nobody is doing that. It's arising of its own accord. And that's the last thing the mind wants to hear! You see, the mind will never be satisfied with any intellectual answer. If I say there *is* an individual, or if I say there *isn't* one, the mind will still try and work it all out. The point isn't to work it all out, but to see this, in clarity. And then all questions drop.

Q. There's a sense of hereness, and in that, there's a certain amount of history. But the history plays itself out, doesn't it? Essentially, the hereness is what's really happening.

Yes, and the history only arises as a thought. And when the thought isn't there, the history isn't there.

Q. And we can draw upon the history if we need it.

Yes, if it arises.

Q. Yes, and it's part of the hereness.

There are no mistakes. Not even the possibility of that. To the individual, though, there can be mistakes. In this hereness, as you put it, it's all as it is. *As it is.* And there's nothing out of place in that. And it takes this form now.

Q. Yes. When you get on your bike, or when you get in the car.

Or when you get on *his* bike!
(Laughter)

Q. But there's no separation is there? There's just the *sense* of separation. And when that sense comes up, it's in the realm of feeling. But that's felt by the hereness. It's experienced by whatever is here. Is that right? Is there an experiencing of it?

The mind comes in and *calls* it a sense of separation. Actually there's no sense of separation.

Q. It's as it is.

Yes.

Q. It's a label.

Yes. The illusion is that there is somebody here who is experiencing the separation.

Q. But there is an experience?

Okay, this is the problem with language! When you're in the world of language, you're in the world of duality. The *experience* and the *experiencer* arise together. So really, in language, you cannot talk about an experience without an experiencer, and vice versa. The experience arises with the one who experiences.

Q. Does there *have* to be an experiencer?

It's the experiencer who creates the experience. Without the experiencer, there's no experience. There's no way of knowing what's going on. There's no way of knowing that there's an experience. You have to *tell* yourself that you're having an experience. You have to tell yourself that you're hearing, you're seeing, you're touching. Without that, you have no way of knowing what's going on. I have no way of knowing if I'm experiencing this or not. Of course, thought can come in and say "I'm experiencing this". But it's just a thought. Without that thought, really nothing is happening. You have no words for it.

~

Q. Without the label "separation", there's still a consciousness there, isn't there? Does a baby have consciousness?

Well, nobody *has* consciousness. It cannot be possessed. There's just what's happening. To the baby, that's all there is. And then we give the baby a name, and we load our expectations onto it, and before long there's a little adult there, with a strong sense of identity. And with that, a strong sense of separation. Identity and separation are the same movement of thought.

Q. But initially, in the case of the newborn baby, there's still a conscious being there, isn't there?

We can use so many words like *consciousness*, and *awareness*, and *being*. And we can get so lost in our theories and concepts, and trying to work out if we *have* consciousness, or if we *are* conscious, or if we can have it and then lose it, and so on. The point is, for a newborn baby, there isn't yet a strong sense of identity. There is just an openness to the world, and with that, an innocence and a wonder.

And of course, we can't *really* talk about what babies

experience. You know, those are still theories, still just our ideas, our projections. The point is that undeniably as adults we lose that sense of childlike wonder, that spontaneity. We become separate. And we miss what's happening. We miss *this*.

Q. Is *this* wholly visible? Or is some of it hidden?

Nothing is hidden. It is constantly in plain view. There is nothing behind the appearance.

Q. Nothing going on behind the scenes?

No. There is no "behind". That's still part of the dream world of duality. Appearance and behind-the-appearance. Visible and invisible.

It's all One. In Oneness, nothing is hidden, nothing is out of place. It is all given.

Q. It's extraordinary. There's nothing behind the scenes, and yet it's coming out with all this stuff!

That's the absolute mystery of life. Out of nothing, everything happens. And it's what we are. It's right at the heart of what we take ourselves to be. The mystery isn't out there, it's right here.

And every morning the eyes open, and a world appears. And we move so far away from that simplicity, from the extraordinary fact that this is happening *at all*. It's so extraordinary, and yet we move so far away from that in our search, in our desperation to become someone in the world. But this simplicity is absolutely free. It doesn't matter how young or old you are, what colour you are, what religion you are. That's why some people have called it unconditional love. It's free. It asks nothing of you. Or they call it grace, which actually, if you look it up in the dictionary, means "an unmerited or undeserved gift from God"! It's undeserved! Unmerited! Which means, this freedom constantly happens in spite of what we do, or don't do, to earn it!

But we put so many demands on this freedom. We draw up so many shopping lists: how we need to change, how we need to purify ourselves, to be good, and so on, in order to see this. No, freedom is absolutely free, and there are no requirements. We think we'll see this "one day", and "one day" never comes!

Q. It's a shame that, isn't it!
(Laughter)

No, it's a gift! Because you know, "one day" is already happening. And today is the day! That's the point. It's already happening.

Oneness is so well hidden that it's appearing, right now, as *everything*, literally *everything*, and yet we *still* can't see it!

Q. In language, I get that this is it. In actuality, getting that this is it, is much harder!

Yes, if you understand this intellectually, all you're left with is an intellectual understanding. You're just a person with an intellectual understanding. So what? It doesn't change anything. This is about a *seeing*, not an intellectual understanding. And in that seeing, all seeking and suffering falls away, and then you don't even *care* anymore about any sort of intellectual understanding!

Q. I understand that it's beyond understanding!
(Laughter)

Q. But *there* is where the confusion starts.

So stay with the confusion, if it's there. The confusion can be very powerful. You see, the confusion is the truth. It's the mind not getting what it wants. It's pointing to the painful truth that ultimately the mind can never have what it wants.

Q. And when it doesn't get what it wants, it gets tired. Like it needs to sleep or something.

Yes, it exhausts itself.

Q. It's too much for the mind to take on.

And then there's a collapse into an ease that's totally beyond the mind. And then you can just sit back and sunbathe in this.

Q. When I was eight years old, I went through a period

of extreme suffering. I was quite lucky in a way. One night I was sitting in bed in the middle of the night, and it became so painful, and suddenly my entire thought structure collapsed. And back then I didn't know what it was. I didn't analyse it or intellectualise it. It collapsed, and then there was just a sense of relief, and a sense that this had *always* been.

Yes, this whole structure of thought can seem so real. And then, in a moment, it's gone. That's how fragile it all is. And actually, every night it falls away. It's so fragile.

Q. I had an experience where thought just fell away. And then the mind came back in, and I started looking for the experience again, wondering what had happened to me and so on. And that's how I lost it.

Yes, the mind comes back in and wonders what happened. It wants to understand what happened so it can control it. To the mind, understanding and controlling are the same thing.

Q. My mind just thought it was great! And I wanted it back, but it wasn't there.

The moment you look for it, it's not there. And yet you can't even call it an experience, you can't really say that you had it and you lost it, because really there was nobody there at the time. There was nobody there to know it as an experience. It becomes an experience in hindsight. The mind comes back in, and says "something happened to me". That's the experience. The experience is a story.

To the mind, what actually happened there was very threatening! The absence of you is a very threatening thing. To the mind, it's death. Death of the individual self. And so inevitably it will start seeking again. It doesn't want to accept that in the absence of you, things could possibly be okay! It doesn't want to see the freedom there. And so it starts seeking. It pretends that it needs to "get this back", in order to keep itself alive. And it kids you that it's not seeking. Of course it's seeking! That's all it can do! It's what the mind does, and it does it perfectly.

Q. My mind makes me worry about things that aren't happening, in order to keep itself going. Worrying about things that aren't remotely important in my life.

So isn't it obvious that you aren't doing that?

Q. But that's difficult to hear. It's a bit of a bugger, isn't it?

It's a problem if you're looking for it to be something that it's not. That's the suffering, really. The thought itself is just a thought. Just a picture. Just a dream.

You know, this seeking game just plays itself out. It exhausts itself, eventually. Everything does, eventually, that's the nature of this manifestation. Things arise, dance around for a while, and pass on.

Q. But there's a fear that if I forget to search, I might get lost in thought again.

Oh, that's the beauty of this, you don't have to *do* anything. There's no requirements here. The point is, it's already being done. It's being done. It's *not* that there's nothing you can do. It's that it's already being done. It's arising now as breathing, and thoughts arising, and that question being asked!

Look at an ant. For an ant, there is no search, no separation, no heavy psychological burden, and look at how perfectly it functions! And yet we humans are so scared to lose this burden, because we think that the Universe cannot function without us! What arrogance! What narcissism! There is an intelligence happening here that's absolutely beyond our understanding.

(Pause)

You see, the moment you have an idea of how *this* should be, that's the search, that's the suffering.

Q. Well, I don't think I have an expectation of how it should be, I mean here in this room. Perhaps I have a feeling that I'm not being all that I can be, I mean in terms of other peoples' judgements.

And that's the same thing. We are your story. We are part of your dream. "Other people" are part of your dream. It's all One.

Q. It's a good dream!

And the waking up from the dream, is the seeing of the dream *as* a dream. As a story arising now. It has no more solidity than that.

Q. What is the meaning of life?

To be here. Asking that question. Breathing. That's it.

Q. Is that my purpose?

There is no other.

(Pause)

Q. It's already fulfilled, isn't it?

Of course. It's already complete, in itself. It needs nothing more.

You know, if you ever want to know where you should be, just look at your feet. Your purpose in life is to be wherever your feet are.
(Laughter)

It's never more complicated than that. Follow your feet. You never know where they'll take you next. And when it's seen that they're not even "your" feet... well, that's the end of it. Your feet always show you where Home is. That's the secret.

And the secret isn't just in the feet. *Everything* is pointing back Home. Everything is trying to wake you up, to show you that you never left Home in the first place. Everything exists for that reason and that reason alone: to wake you up. Even the most intense suffering is there to wake you up. And when that is seen in absolute clarity, there is no "suffering" anymore to wake up from! There is just what's happening. There is suffering, but nobody there who suffers... and therefore no suffering at all! And there is no contradiction there, not at all.

But until this is seen, suffering will be experienced *as* suffering. When suffering is seen through, there is no longer any suffering, because there's nobody there to suffer! But suffering will carry on pummelling the apparent individual until this is seen. It will pummel you as hard as it needs to, until you wake up, until the idea that you're *an individual who suffers* just dissolves.

This is the secret hidden in the midst of suffering, the secret *right at the heart* of suffering. Suffering is always pointing to the end of suffering, to the non-existence of the one who suffers. At the heart of the crucifixion, there is Eternal Life.

The mind hasn't a hope of understanding this. Trying to understand these words will only ever leave confusion. But somewhere beyond that mental confusion there can be a resonance with what is being said, and it's like "oh yes, I've always known this. Right from the beginning I've known this. I can't put it into words, but somehow this has always been known, and somehow this is what I am, and somehow it's all okay."

And that resonance is such a relief. After a lifetime of seeking, it's such a relief. That resonance is the bonfire that burns up all seeking, leaving a silence and a clarity beyond mind. We throw our questions and answers onto this bonfire and they burn up, they just burn up.

~

Q. You say there's a "waking up", which implies time. Does time come into play?

Well, the moment you say it, yes, of course. Language operates in the field of time and space. So the moment you utter the words "waking up", the mind asks "when?". When using language, we are dealing with the dream world of time and space. When using language to talk about this, we're doomed, really.

Q. We're doomed from the start though, aren't we? We're apparent separate human beings, sitting here and listening to what you have to say, and so already we're lost in that world.

Oh, there's no mistakes. If you're here, that's *what is*. That's the freedom right there. Wherever you are, that's it, that's exactly where you should be. Until you find yourself walking out. But there's no way of knowing now. You might walk out of the room in the next ten seconds, but there's no way of knowing now. Even if you know now that you're going to walk out, you might not walk out.

So the only suffering is the story of choice. When that goes, *this* is all that could possibly be happening, because

I couldn't have chosen otherwise. That's the freedom, right there. Without the story of choice, it's just being done.

Q. So I can know that? There is a knowing...

The knowing is what you are. There's always been that knowing.

Q. So, someone like Ramana Maharshi for example, he's just someone you read about, it happened in the past and it's just a story happening now. But that person inspires us.

Until you don't need them anymore. When the need is there, the teacher will appear. When the need goes, there are no longer any teachers, there's just what's happening. So you see, this is part of your dream. The seeker creates the teachers. The seeker creates Ramana Maharshi, so he can be reminded that he doesn't need Ramana Maharshi, and that the whole world is just a story. As long as you need a teacher, he'll be there. And when the seeking dies, there's no more teachers.

Q. And you appeared here tonight?

Yes. You see, there's a perfect balance to this. Needs are always met. The Jeff Foster character arose to meet your need. When the need is no longer there, I disappear. And I stop being a teacher and become what I always was: a friend. And then you are only ever meeting yourself.

Our needs are always met, but never in the way we imagined they would be.

~

Q. If we all spoke different languages, and none of us understood what anyone else was saying, there would just be a being together, wouldn't there? There wouldn't be an understanding of the words, but there would be a meeting, a meeting in being.

Yes, and that's all that's happening here. It's all that's ever happening. Not just in this room, but everywhere. It's always a meeting in Oneness. It's Oneness meeting itself and delighting in that.

Q. Words are just a pretext, aren't they?

Really this is just noise!
(Laughter)

As long as there is seeking, these words will mean something. When the seeking dies, this is just noise. It's equal to the barking of a dog or the miaowing of a cat. It's absolute equality.

Q. Yes. And even if the seeking has exhausted itself, there may be a residue of seeking that's playing itself out?

Absolutely. It plays itself out. Until it doesn't anymore. But there's no way of knowing what will happen!

~

Q. When you say that seeking exhausts itself, it sounds like a story to me, and I wonder if it's actually true.

Oh, nothing I say is true! *(Laughter)*

It's all a story. It appears as though there is seeking, and there is the end of seeking. And somehow it plays itself out. And of course that's just a story we're telling now. Everything is, really.

Q. Are you suggesting that at some point in the *future*, the seeking will end?

That's how it might be heard. Anything I say could be used to form some sort of future goal. "The end of seeking" just becomes another goal.

In the story of Jeff, there was seeking, which became more and more intense, and then fell away. And that's a common story.

Q. But it can happen without the intense seeking?

Of course. But really everyone is seeking. The mind is a seeker. That's what it is. It seeks because it feels separate. And whether its goals are spiritual or material, it's the same movement happening. Whether we use alcohol or meditation to quiet the mind, to lose ourselves, to obliterate the heaviness of being a separate self, it's all just part of our search to come home. It's Oneness looking for itself.

Q. So the search just exhausts itself?

Oh, everything does, eventually. And the mind exhausts itself now, or a moment before death. At some point, the seeking has to end, that's its nature.

Q. So it may never exhaust itself in a person's life?

Even then, at the moment of death, it's over. That's why death is liberation.

Q. But some people die in incredible suffering.

And that would only ever be your story. There's no way of knowing what they are experiencing.

You see, at the moment of death, all seeking, all suffering ends. It's a plunge into the Unknown, which is where we always are. It's where we are now.

So really, there is no death. That's just our story. When it's seen that you are not alive, it's seen that you cannot die. And the death of others is just your own projection. As long as there is someone *here*, there will be someone *there*. When the person *here* goes, the person over *there* goes too. And then there's no death.

This isn't to condemn seeking. Seeking is really Oneness looking for itself, trying to come home to what it is. And in that, it's not a problem. It's only a problem for the person who wants to be free from it. It's the hardest thing to hear, but actually seeking is identical with the effort to end the seeking. Seeking, and seeking the end of seeking, are one.

Q. Sometimes, as a distraction, the mind even seeks suffering.

Oh yes. Suffering gives you an identity.

Q. And maybe it will get to the end of the search through the suffering.

You know, suffering always points to another possibility. It points to the end of suffering.

Suffering is the resistance to what is, so it's constantly pointing to the ending of that resistance. Everything points towards its own end. The end of suffering is *through* the suffering.

Q. Some teachers say that one gets realised through suffering. So then it seems like a bugger if you're not suffering enough! *(Laughter)*

Everyone has the right amount of suffering for their own realisation! Your amount of suffering is the perfect amount for you! There are no mistakes in Oneness. It's all your own dream, anyway.

Q. In my life, I've had this idea that people are asleep, and I don't want to be like them, so I want to wake up.

And they are just your story. They are you. There's no separation. It's because there's someone who's asleep *here* that it gets projected out *there*. It's all a projection. So when the sleeping person *here* goes, the sleeping person over *there* goes too. When the violence *here* goes, the violence *there* goes too.

Q. Yes, I get that. In my life, certain things I've just given up, and then I've realised that other people are suddenly free from those things as well.

Yes, it's amazing, isn't it? It's all your dream, your projection. And when thought isn't there, the dream isn't there either.

Q. Yes. And there's a great peace in that. Just to see it as a thought.

It's always just a thought.

Q. In each and every life, right from the word go, there's an energy that seems to be moving towards resolution. The unfolding of a life, is a kind of constant movement towards resolution. And the unfolding of suffering seems to be a part of that.

Suffering speaks of another possibility: that perhaps there is nobody there who is suffering. That's the astonishing thing about suffering. There can be the most intense pain, the most intense suffering, and right at the heart of that suffering, there's nobody there experiencing it. Right at the heart of suffering, there is just openness. Just love. And it's all playing itself out, as it must.

Q. When we speak about people dying in dire circumstances, we're always on the outside looking in. You were saying before that we can't actually know what's being experienced there.

Yes. Really there's no entity there who dies. From the outside it could appear as though there's someone there who's suffering intensely. But actually it's happening for no one, whether or not it's seen as such. But really, everything we say about dying people, it's just our story. We cannot know.

Q. It's like on the news on TV. There's some terrible stories out there. To the viewer, it can evoke horror and sadness.

Well, we see our *own* suffering. When it's seen that nobody is suffering, that doesn't mean that you do nothing to help. On the contrary, so much energy is freed up that you can be a great help to mankind. You do what needs to be done. Whether that's helping an old lady across the road, or feeding the cat, or trying to save the planet. You help, because you are no longer separate from anything that arises. The point is, there's no way of knowing what will happen, or what you'll do.

Q. Yes, it seems to move towards things that aren't as awake. You're not frightened to move towards things that scare other people.

Yes, when there's nothing left here anymore, there is just an openness for that. And there can be a movement to be of service. But there's no fear in it anymore, because there's no longer anything to defend. And there's certainly no way of knowing where it will take you.

Q. You're not doing it to be a martyr.

Exactly.

Part Two

Q. What I find these days is that I'm not doing anything for a result. But there is still mind-talk, at times.

Oh, there's supposed to be! Whatever is arising right now, is all that could possibly be arising. That's the freedom. It's the person who comes in and says "I don't want what's happening to be happening", that's the suffering, that's the search. You're tearing yourself in two. Me versus life. Me versus my thoughts.

Q. But quite often that's not apparent, is it? That there's a "no" to life happening.

Actually the "yes" and the "no" to life are really the same thing. They are equally powerless over life! Life happens – look, it's happening now – and we say "no" or we say "yes". Still, it happens. That's the beauty of this. You don't have to go round saying "yes" to everything.

Q. Or you could say "yes" to your "no"!

Or "no" to your "yes"!
(Laughter)

~

Q. I hate anger.

What anger is showing you, and in fact what everything is showing you, is that there is no choice. You wouldn't choose to get angry if you could help it. It's not particularly pleasant. People talk about anger just overtaking them, you know. You wouldn't choose it, if you had the choice. You would deal with the situation efficiently and effectively, but without the anger and without the heaviness. When anger overtakes you, it stops you from seeing clearly. I think we all have a sense of this.

Actually, there is no anger. There is just aliveness. And the mind comes in, and says "I am angry. I am a person who's experiencing anger". *That's* the anger. *The anger is the story of anger.* Without the story, there's no way of knowing what's going on. There's just the aliveness of it, just the energy of it, and it has no name. You simply don't know what's happening. It's the divine mystery, and the mind comes in and calls it anger, and with that, you get an identity. It becomes a solid, heavy thing. You take freedom, and put a boundary there, and it happens in the blink of an eye.

And then the game begins. You become an angry *person*. And then you start looking for reasons, causes, justifications. "He made me angry. He did it to me. It's his fault. What can I do in retaliation?" So you're caught up in the world of cause and effect. You're lost in a search, a search to do something about this illusory anger, which isn't even there! That's where the violence comes from: *deep down, you know the anger isn't there.* So you have to pretend it's there, and lash out at the world. You have to keep your illusion alive, by any means necessary. You're trying to keep *yourself* alive, and using anger to justify that. That's the suffering.

Q. So it begins with anger, and then it becomes "I am angry"?

252

There can be anger, and it can be seen with absolute clarity that there is nobody there who is angry. It can be seen that the anger does not belong to anyone. And in that, the anger is still allowed to play itself out. The anger is allowed to be angry. Don't try and understand this intellectually! Go to your own experience. Have you ever been angry, so angry, and then you've become distracted, and the anger has disappeared totally? Then you've had a taste of what I'm talking about. The anger is so fragile, because it's built on the illusion of individuality. The illusion that there is a solid "me" at the centre of my life.

So, it can be seen with absolute clarity that there is no person who is angry (or sad, or jealous, or fearful): there is just the anger, playing itself out in an open space. And actually, you can't even know that! It's just aliveness. And actually without the attempt to end anger, anger is quite exciting. It's very alive. And then the violence goes out of it. And this applies to any emotion, not just anger. It's all the search for an *identity*. And in the absence of that search, everything is freed and everything unravels.

The end of anger is *through* the anger. It's not through an *escape* from the anger. That's the suffering, that's the violence. You carry your cross, and you die into the cross, and God meets you there, and all is forgiven. And this is the true message of the cross: the separation is sacrificed, and God reveals himself. Jesus knew this. He was trying to tell us this.

Q. I always thought that anger is a signpost back home.

Everything is, yes.

Q. Like it's pointing *this* way.

Yes. Everything just wants to be *seen*. The anger just wants to be *seen*. We think we need to do something with it, but really in doing something with it we're just fuelling it.

Anger isn't yours. And in the seeing of that, it withers and dies, in its own time, because it's no longer directed outwards. It's no longer trying to attack the outside world. And it's no longer directed inwards, at an illusory "me". It just hangs there in mid-air, lives its little life, and dies when it's ready. And it's not a problem. This is the end of violence.

Everything just wants to be seen. And in the simplicity of that seeing, *anger is there, and yet it's not there.* It's allowed to be there, and yet on closer inspection, it's empty, it has no substance at all. *Fully there, fully absent.* And this seems to be a paradox to a mind trying to work it all out. "How can it be fully there, and fully not there?" The poor old mind hasn't a hope of understanding this!

So, in this seeing, everything is released. Anger is released. It can be itself, fully. Anger can be anger! Sadness can be sadness! But there's no longer anyone there *doing* anger or *doing* sadness. And actually there never was anyone there in the first place.

Q. Jeff, that's a profound insight, isn't it?

It's shocking. When it's seen, it's shocking.

Q. I mean, so many people throughout history have caused mayhem by being angry. To come to a point where

they see that it's just as it is, that's a profound insight.

But it can happen.

Q. Yes, but it's profound. I mean, not many people have seen this.

Well, it *has* to be that way. The game of individuality goes on, until it doesn't. This will be seen when it's seen. And it can be seen any time, any place. In the middle of the most intense suffering, this can be seen.

Q. Yes, I go into prisons and teach yoga. And you hear the stories of people there who have seen anger, and what it's done to them, and it's profoundly moving. By being locked up in prison, sometimes that provides a way for them to wake up to this seeing. Sometimes they wake up to what you're talking about. And they go "Oh! That's what it is. That's what anger is like!" Before that, they could be overtaken by anger in a microsecond. Now they just see it for what it is. Still, it's very human to want to *do* something with anger, isn't it?

Oh, absolutely! Do something with anger, if you feel that's what you need. We're not rejecting any of that.

Q. Recently we bought a house, and the neighbours from hell moved in!
(Laughter)

Q. There's a lot of noise. And sometimes, lying in bed at

night listening to it, there can be great anger. It's really interesting to see how it just wells up like that.

And what's wrong with being angry, if that's what's arising in the moment?

Q. It's the mind not wanting the anger to be there. It needs to get rid of the anger before it can sleep!

If you are *fully* angry, there is no anger. It destroys it. It burns it all up.

Q. Yes. To go all the way with it.

It burns itself up.

Q. And then you can breathe.

Yes.

Q. Isn't anger just the mind not wanting things to be as they are? Even waiting in a queue sometimes, I get really angry. It's a reaction to things not being the way you want them to be.

Well, that's how it appears. Actually, it's not a *reaction*. The story of a "reaction" is the mind's attempt to justify the anger. So, say, something isn't going the way I wanted it to. That *is* the anger. The anger isn't a *reaction* to that. The anger *is* that. It wasn't *caused* by that. It *is* that. They are the same.

Actually, we never get angry *at* anything. That's the story. That's the justification. That keeps the anger alive. Let me give you an example. Here's a good story. Your angry relative is shouting at you. She's very angry at something you've done. And it's making you angry. But because there's no separation, her anger *is* my anger. So the anger *here*, is the anger *there*. The anger here *is* the angry relative. Can you see this?

But what we do is carry that anger away with us! The angry relative goes away, and we are left with the anger, which is actually her anger, in the story anyway, and we keep that anger alive by continuing to tell the story "she made me angry".

Q. Still, you are part of the anger that is taking place?

Anger is happening. It's not *mine* or *hers*. It's being thrown up by the Universe. It's a play of Oneness, and nobody is doing it. And when there's nobody there trying to grasp that anger anymore, trying to manipulate it, the anger is released and dissolves back into the Universe. And the violence goes out of the situation, and there can be a clear and sane response, coming from a place of clarity.

Q. So you feel angry when she starts shouting at you?

That *is* the anger. It's not that you feel angry *at* her.

Q. So what about the anger at the noisy neighbours?

The anger *is* the noise.

(Pause)

Q. Oh! I just had an *a-ha* moment!

Q. I'm working in prison at the moment. Every day, the fury that I see! I get used to it though, and it becomes almost like a movie. There's fury there, and the next moment it's over. It plays out just like a movie, just like you were saying. And I just let it burn itself out.

Yes, it's just a movie. This is a cartoon world.

Q. Sometimes when we're walking our dog, we encounter a very hostile lady. She's very strange, very wrapped up in her story, very aggressive. She's taken a great dislike to our dog, and to us. We've never done anything to her. It's a learning experience for us to be with her, without getting involved in it.

You know, this is given to you, so it can be seen. Life doesn't want you to *do* anything about it. Just to *see* it in clarity. And in that seeing, the whole thing can fall away, and then you meet that lady for the first time. And you no longer know who or what she is. You meet her in Oneness, and you are both joined there, and out of that there can be a sane response to her ranting and raving, because you are her and she is you, and she is *given* so this can be seen.

Q. Yes.

The suffering is trying to *solve* this, as if it were a problem that needed to be solved. The *seeing* of it ends it. She's a cartoon lady walking a cartoon dog, with cartoon hostility. Just a lady and her dog, and the occasional outburst of anger. It's not your anger, and it's not hers. It's not your problem to solve. In the seeing of this, the problem falls away, and you meet the dog lady for the first time.

～

Q. Sometimes when I get angry, I try to allow the anger, but it doesn't always work for long.

Why should you allow it? Who told you to allow the anger? You see, that's what's fuelling the anger.

Q. What is?

The attempt to escape anger. That's fuelling the anger. Fuelling the sense that you're an angry *person*, when really there's just the aliveness of what's happening, just the energy of it, with no solid "me" at the centre. Anger is already happening for no one.

Q. The attempt to escape it is fuelling it?

Yes, and even *allowing* it is a subtle attempt to *escape* it. Allowing implies *future*.

Q. The allowing is trying to escape it too?

Yes.

Q. So what to do?

You see, anger doesn't want you to do anything with it.

Q. How about softening around it?

Have you tried softening? Has it worked?

[Laughter]

So, anger arises. *Now.* What do you do with it?

Q. Various things. Sometimes I express it. Sometimes I'm aware of it. Sometimes I try to relax around it.

Look, the reason you can't do anything with the anger, is because it's not there.

Q. It's not there. But it seems like a situation has arisen. And yet it's not there?

Give me an example.

Q. A man bullied me in the swimming pool. I was in the wrong lane, and he swam into me and told me to move. I was angry.

Do you think he had a choice?

Q. *(Pause)* No. It's just what was happening.

And you didn't have a choice either. You didn't choose to get angry at this. This all unfolded in innocence. The guy bumped into you in innocence, and anger arose for you in innocence. Neither of you were doing this. And the seeing of that ends the anger. And in that, there can be a dealing with whatever arises. You don't have to take his anger away with you.

And that's why you've been given this guy.

Q. So I can see it.

Yes, everything is for that. He's part of your dream, you see. The poor guy, he's not even *here*! It's like, he's there and he's gone, in a flash. And you keep telling the story of the guy in the swimming pool, and you keep him alive. The poor guy, he could be dead by now. He could have been run over by a steamroller. And yet we keep him alive, out of our own need for an identity.

Q. I'm not keeping him alive. I just haven't gone back to the swimming pool!
(Laughter)

Well, that's one way of doing it!
(Laughter)

He's probably there waiting for you!

Q. I just haven't gone back there for a swim.

Yes, and next time you do, you can go up to him and thank him for bumping into you and jarring you into clarity!

∾

Q. I feel angry now. I was trying to get it, but I lost it. It feels like suffering.

Be there with the anger. It stays for a while, and passes. Everything does. Right now, there's anger. That's what is.

Q. Yes. The anger is wanting things to be different, isn't it? It's almost like the anger is okay, but there's this other bit that goes "oh there you go, getting angry again!"

Yes, anger at anger.

Q. It's like, if I was more awake, this wouldn't be happening!

Yes, that's a common one!

Q. Wow. It's amazing how easily that happens.

Then anger is your teacher. It's what you've been given so that you can wake up and see it for what it is.

Q. Yes, that's a good point. It's seeing, in the moment of the anger, that nobody is choosing it. No, it's just happening.

Exactly. Would you have chosen the anger, if you'd had the choice?

Q. No.

So you're innocent. There's no choice. That's why I say this is all happening in innocence.

~

Q. So there's an inevitability about everything that happens?

Yes, but only because it happens. Not because it was *destined* to happen.

~

Q. Going back to the dog lady. One day, when she was abusing me verbally, I tried to interact with her in a loving way.

Oh, she couldn't care less!

Q. Yes, you're right. She couldn't care less. Absolutely! And I saw that. Then I tried being rude, and she got worse. So I saw that she really was something else! There was nowhere to go. Each time I've encountered her I've been presented with this opportunity to see anger playing itself out.

Her anger is your anger.

Q. Her anger, which she's generating for whatever reason, is my anger. There's only one anger.

Yes, there's only one anger. And it's not her fault. And it's not your fault. When that's seen, it goes.

Q. The moment I call it her fault, I make it worse.

And in the seeing of that, she can carry on doing what she does. She's allowed to carry on being herself fully, and she has no choice in it.

Q. She's doing what she does. She's being what she is. [Pause] Actually I saw the dog lady the other day. And it was okay. I just saw her for what she was, and I didn't carry it with me afterwards.

Yes. The anger at the dog lady is the suffering. And actually, the dog lady *is* the anger. They are not separate. Your anger is the dog lady. She isn't causing anything. That's the wheel of suffering right there. To see the anger over *here* as just anger, arising for no one, is to release her as well. And in that, she can continue to be the dog lady! Like a character in a story. Like a cartoon.

Q. So we can actually just enjoy this story. It's a real learning experience. It's very helpful, what you're saying. An encounter with raw anger. To encounter a very extreme manifestation of anger is interesting.

To see the anger as just presently arising energy, is freedom. It's just arising of its own accord. It's not caused by anything. The story of cause and effect is the story of suffering. "You did this to me!" That's the beginning of violence. But it's just Oneness *anger*-ing. And that releases it from the shackles of cause and effect, blame, resentment and so on.

And that means that anger can be fully angry! This isn't about denying anger, suppressing it, and so on. We've tried that for thousands of years, and it hasn't worked!

~

Q. So anger isn't caused?

That's the justification. That's how we keep the anger going. "You caused my anger". But until it's seen that it's not caused, it's very much caused!

Q. But it's not about blaming yourself either, right?

Blaming yourself and blaming others is the same movement.

Q. But anger doesn't just come out of nowhere. I don't just sit here and get angry. Something happens and then anger arises. So it's caused by something, isn't it?

The point is, you don't have the choice. You don't choose to get angry. Nobody would choose to suffer, if they had the choice.

Q. Or make somebody angry?

Yes. In that sense, it arises out of nowhere. And *then* we tell the story of how, and why, and so on. And we get lost in that. And that fuels it.

To see it as just energy arising, for no one, is to end it. It just offers itself. And it's not mine and it's not yours. And it's not caused by you or me. It's just part of what's happening.

And it might not be here in the next moment! But it's here now. It's a welcome friend.

Q. So is anger necessary?

Everything that is arising is necessary.

Q. Necessary for awakening?

Yes. There's an idea that anger isn't "spiritual". That's a load of crap.

Q. So people need this anger to be identified as a human being?

Yes, it's like we don't want to stop being angry at *them*, because then we lose *our* identity as "the victim" or "the angry person". We don't want to lose the anger. When I'm angry, I know who I am. I'm an angry person! It's safe. It's known.

Q. Yes, it's like some people with depression, wake up one morning and they feel fine, and they don't know what to do! It's a new feeling. Up until that point the depression has defined them.

Yes. It's all so hard to let go of. You don't want to lose your identity.

Q. Sometimes I speak to an elderly relative of mine on the telephone, and she cuts me dead. It's hard to deal with. It makes me feel rejected.

And that's why she is cutting you off, so you can see that the "poor me" is just a story! This is what life has given you. So you can see that there is no "poor me" there. And in that, you can go back to her, and she can carry on cutting you off. You see, that's what she needs. She has no choice.

You're giving her what she needs. You wouldn't want to take that away from her. That's not compassion. In the seeing that her suffering is your suffering, you can be there for her, and that might involve being cut off a hundred more times.

Q. So as long as she needs to cut me off, she will.

Yes, she'll carry on cutting you off, until you can see that "she cuts me off" is just a story that you tell in order to stay separate. And then there will be no resistance to what she apparently does to you, because it will be clear that "she" isn't doing *anything* to "you", at all! You'll be on the phone, and then the phone will cut off, and then if the story "she cut me off" still arises, you'll see that she only acted that way because of the *dream* she's having, and it's a dream she hasn't been able to wake up from yet. She has no choice. And that releases it. And then there can be an *okayness* with the phone being hung up. And you walk away from the phone and start doing something else, and there's no residue, it's all just wiped clean.

She's just a woman who cuts you off on the phone. That's all. She's a character in a novel, a character who cuts people off.

Q. My problem with anger is definitely wrapped up in my story about being a "nice person".

Yes, nice people shouldn't get angry!
(Laughter)

But what happens if anger arises? It's then very threatening to your idea of who you think you are. It threatens your "nice person" mythology.

Q. Do you get angry?

Anything can happen here. It's an absolute openness to what is. Anger can happen, sadness can happen, joy can happen. It all plays itself out. It's all just energy, and energy can take millions of forms. There's just nobody here who has any sort of idea about what should or shouldn't arise. There's nobody here who cares anymore. So if anger comes, it's a welcome guest. If tears flow, they have a rightful place here. Nothing is denied. Everything is released to be itself. Everything is allowed to come home.

Q. If you look at the history of the world, it seems that anger is a strong energy in this world. The energy of anger seems to be hard to handle.

And yet there are no mistakes.

Q. Yes, and when you talk about these things, they appear

to be real. There seems to be a fundamental, powerful creative force at work here.

And yet when you go bed at night, the entire world is wiped out. In deep sleep there is nothing. So the history of the world, *where is it?*

Q. It feels like it has some substance to it though. If I think about the rainforests being destroyed, and you're saying it's all perfect...

That doesn't mean that you don't go out and do something about it! The action will arise to match the belief. In the seeing that it's all One... you have no idea where that will take you. In the moment, helping an old lady across the road can be as meaningful, as important as saving the rainforests. If you have an idea of what's important in this world, you may miss the old lady. *He who saves a single life, saves the world entire.* The one is the many, and the many is the one. The old lady is equal to all the rainforests.

So there's no way of knowing where it will take you. And the only reason we say it's perfect is because it couldn't have happened any other way. The unfolding of the world couldn't have happened any other way. It happened exactly as it did. To say it could have been different, that's the illusion, that's the dream.

So we always start where we are right now. And right now, I find myself in this room. This is the world. This is the Universe. I don't see any rainforests here. And that doesn't mean that tomorrow I won't be out saving the rainforests. The point is, there's no way of knowing. And that place of not knowing, is one with the Universe. So really it's the Universe helping itself.

The Universe doesn't need our help. That's the hardest thing to hear. And that doesn't mean that you sit back and do nothing. It's so hard to hear.

Q. Oh, I didn't plan on doing anything!
(Laughter)

Q. I mean, nothing's shown up yet.

Maybe it will. Maybe it won't.

Q. Sometimes I talk to people about this. Perhaps just out of that, something might happen.

Yes, perhaps!

∿

Q. It's difficult to hear that it's perfect as it is. It's so bloody obvious though! It is as it is. But sometimes it's hard to hear that.

It's not supposed to be easy to hear. If it was easy to hear, the world would have heard it by now.

Q. But that's perfect too, isn't it?

Yes. It couldn't be otherwise.

But actually, "perfect" isn't a great word. I don't often use that word. *It is as it is.* Or we could say that it's perfect *in its imperfection.*

Q. I still get angry at ignorance though. I get angry at other people not doing anything to change the world.

Your anger isn't changing anything. It's not doing anything. It's dead. It's stagnant. No action comes from there. The mind goes "If I get angry enough, eventually I'll do something." And the anger at other peoples' stagnation, that's a projection of your stagnation. The point is, what are you doing to change the world? Right now, you're sitting here getting angry at the world. In the seeing that your anger already arises for no one, and that you are not separate from this world that you're imagining, the stagnation is released. Your anger is sapping so much energy! *That's* the anger.

Q. Yes, that's what it feels like.

And all of this stems from the idea that you're a person in the world. Where is the world *now*?

Q. Perhaps there isn't one. Sometimes I consider that all there is, is this. That there wasn't a yesterday or tomorrow.

And there's nothing outside of it. The Universe is happening here, in this. This is the place where everything happens. Including the idea of the Universe.

Q. Yes, it's arising here.

So the question "what can I do to change the world?" burns

up in the seeing of this. And really, that's the change you seek. And out of that can come effortless action to change the world, if that desire is still there. It comes from a place of openness, from a place of not knowing, and that's very powerful, and it can change the world.

Q. I feel that I ought to be thinking about the Universe.

It doesn't need that. It's just a thought. And anyway, feeling that you ought to think about the Universe, is the Universe feeling that it ought to be thinking of itself!

Q. But that's what arises.

Yes. You see, you're not a person *in* the Universe. The Universe arises here.

Q. But it seems real when the taxman comes!
(Laughter)

But that's not happening now. It's just a thought arising now. You see, the whole thing is resolved in the clear seeing that this is all that could possibly be happening. So *this* is what the Universe wants you to be doing. *This* is where the Universe wants you to be. There are no mistakes in this. So right now, sitting here, asking these questions, *that* is saving the Universe.

Q. Yes, I feel that.

And that's it. Nothing else is possible. The mind cannot hear this. That what's happening is the only possibility.

Q. Yes.

This is the Universe unfolding, right before your eyes. This must be right, because it's happening. It's too simple!

Q. I find that things go quiet when I see it that way. But the mind wants to come in and start telling stories.

So let it! They are just stories. The mind is innocent.

Q. It might be innocent, but it's dangerous!

It's not dangerous. It's just doing what it does. It's a story-teller. And once it's all seen as a story, it regains its joy, it loses its heaviness. But we often forget that it's just a story.

Q. People used to sit around a campfire, telling stories.

Yes, and that's really what's happening here. We're sitting round a campfire, telling our stories. We're just storytellers. That's all that's happening here. And everything that happened in your life, it's just a story being told now.

All those things that seemed so serious at the time – in hindsight, they can be quite funny. They lose their heaviness. They are seen as just stories.

Q. It's like it happened to someone else, and not you.

Yes, that's the secret. It's never really happening to you.

Q. So that's why we can get over terrible things?

Yes, eventually they are seen to be stories. They just happened. They aren't good or bad – they just happened. That doesn't mean we forget what happened, or deny what happened, but we see that it couldn't have been any other way.

Q. Often if you tell and re-tell a fearful story, it becomes more and more absurd. And it's much more palatable when it's seen as absurd.

Yes. Everything that happened in the past, it's *gone*. It's so simple. It's *gone*. The whole history of the Universe, it's *gone*.

And we're left right here. Present. Breathing. Heart beating. Sounds happening. Traffic outside. And you're fully absent and fully present. You're an open space in which everything arises, and yet you're not separate from everything that arises. When you talk about it, there appears to be duality. The space in which everything arises, and everything that arises. Actually they are One.

You are nothing and everything. This is nothing and everything. It's emptiness arising as form. It's been pointed at throughout the ages, in a million different ways, in all the religions and spiritual traditions.

And ultimately all concepts fall away. This burns up all concepts. Beyond all concepts, *this* is happening. And it's only when you move away from this mystery that the suffering begins. You move into the story of "me and my problems". But a story is just a story, and you're always left here. Nothing arising as everything. The allowing of all form.

And it's so ordinary. That's the cosmic joke. The mind goes "it can't be this, this is too ordinary!" And you move so far away from the gift of what is. From the simplicity of what is presenting itself now. It might not be presenting this in a moment's time, but it is now. And it's enough.

Q. That's why it's so extremely well hidden. Because it's so extremely obvious!
(Laughter)

Q. It's too close to be seen.

Of course! Oneness is so well hidden that it arises as everything, literally everything, and yet we *still* can't see it!

You know, when I first saw this, it was shocking. The simplicity of it was *shocking*. My spiritual search had become so intense, and I was so lost in all these concepts and ideas about liberation and awakening.

And then I saw this in a chair. A *chair*, imagine that! So ordinary! I realised I'd never seen a chair before. It was shocking, the simplicity of it. The grace of it. And it blew away the seeking game. The chair just sat there, offering itself, freely. It asked nothing of me, and yet it was there, ready to hold me if I wanted to sit down. What grace! It was just presenting itself, in each and every moment, asking nothing of me and yet offering itself freely, and it had been doing that throughout my entire search! It's just that I'd never had eyes to see it! The secret had been in plain view the whole time.

And not just the chair, but the carpet and the ceiling and

the table and the hands and the feet too - it was in every-thing. Everything just radiated freedom. And it had been that way from the very beginning. From before the Big Bang. And it was unconditional love. It denied nothing, not even the seeking. It had even allowed the seeking game to play itself out! It was constant. Unconditional. And yet I hadn't been able to see it, because I'd been looking for it. And yet there was even compassion for that, for the person who thought he was separate. It was all unfolding in the purest innocence.

Q. And did this seeing fade?

The chair became a chair again. The table went back to being a table. Everything was allowed to be itself once again.

There is an old Zen saying: *At first, mountains were mountains and rivers were rivers. Later on, mountains were no longer mountains, and rivers were no longer rivers. Finally, mountains were once again mountains, and rivers were once again rivers.*

Everything is now as it is. And it's always enough.

(Pause)

Q. There's a ladybird crawling on your collar!

Oh, it's the Ladybird of Enlightenment!
(Laughter)

∾ One, One, One ∾

The lamps are different,
But the Light is the same.

So many garish lamps in the dying brain's lamp-shop.
Forget about them.

Concentrate on the essence, concentrate on the Light.

In lucid bliss, calmly smoking off its own holy fire,
The Light streams towards you from all things,
All people, all possible permutations of good, evil, thought,
passion.

The lamps are different,
But the Light is the same.

One matter, one Energy, one Light, one Light-mind,
Endlessly emanating all things.

One turning and burning diamond,
One, One, One.

Ground yourself, strip yourself down,
To blind loving silence.

Stay there, until you see
You are gazing at the Light
With its own ageless eyes.

Rumi

For details of books, audio/video,
meetings and retreats,
visit Jeff Foster's website:

www.lifewithoutacentre.com

Printed in the United States
217494BV00001B/2/P

9 780955 829048